625.19
GRA
Grams, John.

Toy train collecting
and operating.

$16.95

DATE			

BAKER & TAYLOR

P9-CRO-112

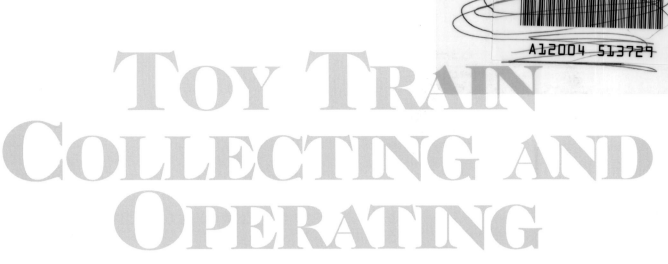

TOY TRAIN COLLECTING AND OPERATING

An Introduction to the Hobby

JOHN GRAMS

KALMBACH
BOOKS

Printed in the United States of America

99 00 01 02 03 04 05 06 07 08   10 9 8 7 6 5 4 3 2 1

For more information, visit our website at
http://books.kalmbach.com
Secure online ordering available

Publisher's Cataloging-in-Publication
(Provided by Quality Books, Inc.)

Grams, John.
    Toy train collecting and operating : an introduction
to the hobby / John A. Grams. — 1st ed.
    p. cm.
    Includes index.
    ISBN: 0-89778-447-2

    1. Railroads—Models—Collectors and collecting
    I. Title.

TF197.G64 1999   625.1´9
                                  QBI98-1057

Book and cover design: Kristi Ludwig

Lionel® is the registered trademark of Lionel L.L.C., Chesterfield, Michigan. This book is neither authorized nor approved by Lionel L.L.C.

CONTENTS

ACKNOWLEDGMENTS

Special thanks to:

John L. Goertz, my grandfather, who labored long and hard in the yards of the Chicago & North Western Railroad, and to his daughter and my mother, Loueen Grams, for introducing me to toy trains before I can remember clearly.

Joshua Lionel Cowen, for publishing the most engrossing and colorful "wish book" catalogs every year.

Generals Dwight D. Eisenhower and Douglas MacArthur, for bringing World War II to a speedy conclusion so that Lionel could resume manufacturing trains before I grew up.

Dick Christianson, for providing the kind of help and encouragement I needed to bring this book into reality.

The staff of *Classic Toy Trains* magazine—Neil Besougloff, Bob Keller, Carl Swanson, and Terry Thompson—for their valuable input and the use of their rich resources.

My train show colleagues and friends—John Heck, Mike Kaye, Joe Pehringer, and John Wickland—for putting up with me on all those Sundays. I learned a lot, guys.

Dave and John Watson, Jack Sommerfeld, and Dwight Ingalls—local guys who shared their trains and their knowledge to improve this book.

Lawrence Luser, Kristi Ludwig, and Lisa Schroeder, whose fine artistry directed these efforts.

Chris Becker, Darla Evans, Art Schmidt, Jim Forbes, and Bill Zuback, for their exquisite photography.

Michael Emmerich, for his work on the first edition, and Roger Carp and Mary Algozin, for their skillful editing and organizing of materials for this edition; Annette Wall and Helene Tsigistras, for patiently seeing this book throughout the production process; and Julie LaFountain, for handling the million trivial and not-so-trivial tasks that go with publishing a book.

Jim Bunte (wherever he may be) for showing me the humor in the human condition. Hang ten, Dude!

And to the hundreds of hi-railers, hot-doggers, semi-scalers, tinplaters, kit-bashers, swap-meet sages, kibitzers, hecklers, and coffee-pot conductors I've met along the way, many of whom have become good friends: thanks for the lift.

John A. Grams
January 1999

A scene from Steve Bales's impressive hi-rail O gauge layout. He runs
Lionel and other stock tinplate trains in a realistic and scale-like setting.

The Many Faces of Railroading

THIS IS A BOOK about toy trains. It is not about precise-scale replicas, hand-crafted miniatures, or artistic interpretations of real trains, but about mass-produced playthings originally intended to delight and amuse children, and marketed as special gifts, which were purported to have the almost magical capability of building and nurturing lifelong bonds between parents and children. Either the selling job was the most successful in history or the toy trains themselves have intrinsic qualities that people still find appealing years after the passing of the golden age of railroading in America.

Today, toy trains are at the center of a rapidly expanding hobby that bridges practically all the demographic and socioeconomic strata. The industry supporting the hobby burgeons with new products and lines, reproductions of old ones, replacement parts, restoration supplies, and a large assortment of cult-like paraphernalia, from bumper stickers to T-shirts. Commerce in both new and used trains is brisk. So this is also a book about people, those who are involved with toy trains on many levels.

There are at least five basic types of "train people" in this part of the world. Although the general public tends to lump them together, it is best for our purposes to keep the categories separate and sharply defined. There may be some who bridge and others who cross over, but the types remain essentially different.

Railfans

The first and undoubtedly the largest group of these train people is made up of railfans. They love trains, the large ones, 1′ = 1′ scale. To them, nothing is more thrilling than a train ride. Or spending hours at the station or the yards, getting caught up in the activity, observing the sights, listening to the sounds, inhaling the odors, soaking up the atmosphere. They hang out in places where railroad employees congregate, hoping to overhear the latest gossip, ask questions, or even share train stories with the pros. When a train passes by, true railfans will be compelled to drop whatever they may be doing and watch.

It is well known that railroading can get into the bloodstream and even the bone marrow of normal humans. Railfans have it in their souls. To them, it is romance, excitement, and a form of addiction more severe than those known to the surgeon general.

Being a railfan at some point in life is a basic prerequisite for entry into the other four train people categories. Without this motivation and experience to draw upon, it would be difficult to maintain an interest in creating, building, operating, controlling, or even owning a collection of miniature trains.

Scale Model Railroaders

Scale model railroaders make up the second group of train people. Their creative interests require a great

Joe Lesser's layout, the JL/ATSF Railway, which uses the Santa Fe as a prototype, is characterized by painstaking attention to even the smallest detail. Joe considers himself more of a scale model railroader than a hi-railer, although he operates his modified ready-made rolling stock on O gauge three-rail track.

diversity of skills, infinite patience, and time frames measured in years. Many scale model railroads are conceived as lifetime projects, which are never finished. They are largely handcrafted, exact-scale, highly detailed miniaturizations of the real world, with railroading as the central focus. Some are patterned after existing railroads (called "prototypes") and locales. Others are period pieces, re-creating scenes and environments in railroad history (steam locomotives are still popular). Regardless of which scale, prototype, locale, or period they prefer or the size of their layout, scale model railroaders share one characteristic: a pride in accomplishment that little else in life can match.

It is impossible to pinpoint when and where this model railroading emphasis began. The first practitioners were probably industrial model makers, engineers, machinists, tinkerers, and electrical experimenters living in the technological boom period after World War I. Because toy trains had been on the market since the turn of the century, it is safe to assume that many scale model railroads evolved from toy train layouts, spurred by the desire of their owners to make the trains more realistic in appearance and operation. In the 1920s, whatever could not be fabricated by modifying toy locomotives and rolling stock had to be built from scratch.

Scale model railroading came of age in the 1930s. Early in the decade, several companies began to serv-ice the hobby, providing car construction kits, accessories, parts, and supplies. National workshop and craft-type magazines regularly ran how-to articles about railroad models, and the hobby spawned a number of periodicals of its own. Many adults became scale model railroaders because they loved trains and perhaps felt foolish about "playing with toys." The skill required to build scale trains alleviated some of the stigma. After all, many model railroaders were out of work and had time on their hands, putting it to good use creating their own perfect world in miniature—a safe haven and retreat from the grim realities of economic depression and later global war.

Recognizing another potential market, the major

Dave Watson's O gauge layout is an excellent example of the traditional type, set up over a layer of green indoor-outdoor carpeting. He obviously loves long trains and operating accessories.

toy train manufacturers produced items targeted at the scale modelers in the years right before World War II. Lionel put out two streamliners, a Hudson, and a switch engine in ¼-inch scale for O gaugers, and a small line in OO for those who had to conserve space. Meanwhile, A.C. Gilbert/American Flyer offered several HO sets and then retooled the entire line to 3⁄16-inch scale, paving the way for conversion to S gauge after the war. This emphasis on realism—or at least scale proportions—changed the look of American toy trains forever.

By the end of the 1930s, scale model railroaders had many choices. Model railroad clubs sprang up in the major American cities. Parts, kits, and ready-made models were plentiful. Standard and the larger gauges were out. By far the most popular scale was O, although the inroads made by the smaller HO and OO trains had many modelers rethinking their use of available space. Then World War II brought all of it to a crashing halt for almost four years.

After the war, scale model railroading shifted emphasis toward the smaller trains. HO became the reigning scale, not only because of advances in technology and in the art of miniaturization, but for the practical reason that postwar houses were smaller. N and Z scales, which are even smaller, were in the experimental stages. Meanwhile, the leading toy train companies continued producing "big trains for little hands": Lionel in O gauge and Gilbert/American Flyer in S (which was only slightly smaller than O). The rift between scale model railroaders and toy train enthusiasts widened, eventually causing a split. Scale modelers became their own distinct classification of train people.

HI-RAILERS

Some toy train operators continued to try to make the transition to exact scale, but many just gave up. The term "hi-railer" was coined in the 1940s for those operators who built layouts that combined elements of both scale and toy railroading. By that time, the trains themselves had taken on a more realistic appearance, with better detail and proportion. They were appealing to those modelers who did not have the inclination, time, or skills needed to build the trains yet wanted to enjoy having a model railroad. Hi-railer layouts could be constructed quickly, and the trains ran well. This greatly broadened the base of potential train hobbyists.

With the introduction of GarGraves and other prototypical-looking track systems, buildings that required minimal assembly (such as Plasticville), and

quick and easy scenery from the pages of hobby magazines, hi-railers could have the best of both worlds. They could build layouts that emphasized operation in a scenic setting that was at least acceptable to most people. Today, the terms "hi-railer" and "toy train operator" are practically synonymous for more than half of those people involved with toy trains. Together, they constitute our third category of train people.

COLLECTORS AND INVESTORS

By the 1950s, both Lionel and Gilbert/American Flyer were turning out products with new road names and paint schemes each year in the hope of stimulating repeat business. They believed a customer would buy another locomotive or car of a type he already owned if it carried a different road name or livery. They were correct. What they probably did not realize was that they were creating future collectibles and opening up a new dimension to the train hobby, the full impact of which would not be felt for another 15 to 20 years.

The toy train industry mirrored the serious problems faced by real railroads during the 1960s. Both were in economic difficulty and suffered from sagging images. Kids wanted other kinds of toys. By the end of the decade, The A.C. Gilbert Co. had gone out of business and Lionel was foundering. In a last-ditch effort to survive, Lionel leased the rights to produce its trains to a subsidiary of General Mills in 1969.

Whether it was the new perspective of General Mills management, its superior advertising and marketing skills, its cash reserve, a nationwide nostalgia craze, the uncertainty of the inflation-plagued economy, or a combination of these factors, interest in toy trains came back strongly in the 1970s and '80s. But now the emphasis was different. The trains were viewed as nostalgic adult collectibles and as investments, not as mere playthings for children. Of course, prices reflected this change by spiraling upward.

Two new breeds of train people emerged: toy train collectors and toy train investors. Often it was difficult to differentiate them. Both were for the most part affluent adults who lacked the time or skills to become hi-railers or scale model railroaders. When they bought the new products, it triggered something inside. Soon they were hunting through attics, basements, and hobbyshop backrooms in search of the lost treasures of youth and old trains of historical significance. Swap meets sprang up all over the country for the barter and sale of vintage toy trains. The ranks of the clubs and collector associations swelled with new

With Allison Cox, toy train collecting has become a way of life. Here he displays Lionel and Ives Standard gauge accessories as well as Lionel Standard and O gauge trains from the 1920s and '30s.

blood. Toy train collectors and investors brought with them a verve and enthusiasm new to the hobby.

Some collectors built operating "world-in-miniature" layouts, but most did not. Instead, they set up pleasing displays of their trains and accessories, using track plans from old catalogs or magazines. Many erected shelves or cases to show off their collections.

Many people who initially invested in toy trains rather than jewels, precious metals, or other hard substances as hedges against inflation, soon became hooked on the hobby. By and large, they held onto their "investments" because they found that playing with toy trains was more fun than playing with diamonds.

By the 1990s, the toy train had come of age. It had become a respected artifact of American popular culture, suitable for serious study by scholars, who traced its history, mythology, and role in society. Many books and magazines were published that examined toy trains from every conceivable angle. The new trains themselves became better—more scale-like, with state-of-the-art technology and attention to detail that rivaled museum models. In short, toy trains had gained social respectability. Nobody apologized for "playing" with them anymore.

Lionel's Standard gauge Blue Comet is a true classic. Patterned after the Jersey Central fun train that ran between New York and Atlantic City on weekends, it captured the fancy of toy buyers in the 1930s and the admiration of train collectors today.

THE RISE, DECLINE, AND RESURRECTION OF AMERICAN TOY TRAINS

TRAINS BECAME AN integral part of the image of the great American Industrial Revolution. They were giant machines, with men in control, carrying raw materials to smoky forges and noisy factories, delivering finished goods to ports of embarkation, bringing produce and livestock from the hinterlands to feed workers in the expanding urban settlements. These brawny behemoths of the rails cast a decidedly "macho" shadow across the landscape. No wonder they so totally captured the imaginations of boys who couldn't wait to become men, and inspired wanderlust and the call of faraway places in almost everyone.

This cast-iron locomotive and tender, intended to be pulled along floors, is typical of the toy trains that were available at the turn of the century.

TOY TRAINS IN THE BEGINNING

The first toy trains were crude, made of wood, and designed to be pulled along the floor. They appeared on the market in the third quarter of the 19th century, only a few years after the prototype locomotives began scaring horses and polluting the plains with soot and cinders. As the mighty trunk railroads developed and spread from coast to coast, toy trains became more durable and realistic. Manufacturers used cast iron in place of wood because it was capable of presenting better detail. But the trains were still pull toys.

Self-propelled trains that ran on sectional track

were products of the waning years of the 19th century. If elfin magic was involved in their creation, the elves were inhabitants of the Black Forest and not the North Pole. German and other European clock makers switched their manufacturing focus from "coo-coos" to "choo-choos." To this day, key-wound, spring-driven trains are often referred to as "clockwork" toys.

Toy train electrification came about during the first two decades of the 20th century. According to the best available evidence, the first electric trains were also produced in Germany. Several American manufacturers, however, came hot on the heels of the Europeans. By 1901, toy trains with electric motors in them were being manufactured on both sides of the Atlantic.

Power for these early trains was supplied by primitive (and dangerous) wet batteries, which were little more than acid-filled Leyden jars. These later gave way to enclosed storage batteries and dry cells. Reliable house current that could be transformed into low voltages to run trains was available only in major metropolitan areas. For most of the country, such an amenity was a thing of the future.

MAJOR TOY TRAIN MAKERS: THE PIONEERS

Lionel. Joshua Lionel Cowen, inventor and inveterate experimenter, had produced military detonators, developed a reliable electric motor, and worked on improving the dry-cell battery before he built the first Lionel train in his New York City loft in 1901. Actually, it was a motorized gondola car that ran on a circle of track. Cowen had intended to sell it to storekeepers as an animated window display. Soon people were playing with the thing, and a toy empire was born. Before long Cowen was making a line of electrically powered trains and trolley cars.

Taking his cue from the real railroads, Cowen pushed for a standardized track gauge for toy trains manufactured in America. His "Lionel Standard" gauge became the industry norm, effectively freezing out competition from many European companies who were producing trains for export in only the old No. One and No. Two gauges. In 1915 Lionel began making

The legendary Converse trolley of the early 1900s was trackless and had a powerful clockwork mechanism wound by turning the trolley pole.

the smaller O gauge models that would become its main products.

Built largely upon the ingenuity of one man, who surrounded himself with a few well-chosen associates, Lionel became a powerful force in the American toy train market in the years after World War I. Cowen fought and eventually defeated most of his competitors, both foreign and domestic.

Although economic reversals forced the company into receivership for a while during the Depression, Lionel emerged from the toy train production hiatus of World War II in a strong position, the world leader in

Lionel O gauge trains from the World War I era. The electric locomotives were patterned after New York Central prototypes, which were familiar to children living throughout the East, the toy maker's primary market at the time.

Compare the first boxcars produced by Ives (1909, rear), American Flyer (1910, middle), and Lionel (1915, front)

This Lionel Jr. freight set from 1935 offered boys everything they needed to get started: train, track, transformer, and trackside accessories.

the field. The golden age of Lionel trains followed. From the mid-1940s to the late 1950s, Lionel set standards in engineering and marketing that others could only hope to emulate. Annual sales numbered in the millions of units. Profits made stockholders giddy. Lionel's competitors were left far behind, choking on dust.

Nothing is forever, though. As J. Lionel Cowen's influence and leadership in the corporation eroded, so did product quality. When Cowen retired in 1958, his son, Lawrence, remained the figurehead chief executive, but stockholder groups fought each other for control. Cash flowed out of the company, and quality sank even lower.

The toy train business was on the ropes in the 1960s, reflecting the diminished role of real railroads in American life. Kids wanted other kinds of toys. Trains were out; red ink was in. For the Lionel Corporation, attempts at diversification had come too late.

In 1969 the rights to manufacture trains under the Lionel trademark were granted to Model Products Corporation, a subsidiary of General Mills. The newly formed Lionel/MPC division slowly turned the company around by changing marketing strategy and rebuilding Lionel's quality image. Instead of targeting children, Lionel made the adult collector market its

As Lionel prepares to celebrate a century in business, this 2⅞-inch locomotive, patterned after a Baltimore & Ohio tunnel locomotive, reminds us of how far toy trains have come since the 1900s.

This Ives Wide gauge electric locomotive from the 1920s reflects the company's insistence on using sturdy cast-iron construction long after other toy train manufacturers had switched to sheet metal.

main focus. Old favorites from the 1940s and 1950s were brought back, sporting spectacular new paint jobs. Starter sets for youngsters were secondary as Lionel/MPC mined a new mother lode.

In 1973 Lionel production was shifted to another General Mills subsidiary, Fundimensions, where it remained for 12 years. Then in a 1985 corporate reorganization, the cereal manufacturer divested itself of Kenner Parker Toys and Lionel was included in the deal.

Shortly thereafter, Detroit real estate magnate Richard Kughn bought the business and formed Lionel Trains, Inc. He introduced state-of-the-art electronics, along with a number of newly designed items to supplement the large array of golden oldies going back to the 1930s. Under his single-handed leadership the Lionel line flourished for a decade.

Kughn sold the company to Wellspring Associates, an investment group, in 1995. The long heritage and classic tradition continue under the supervision of Wellspring.

Ives. Founded by Edward Ives, this Bridgeport, Connecticut, toy company had been in business for more

than 30 years when it began marketing clockwork track trains in 1901. The Ives electric line came in about 1910. Ives was the first American firm to use colorful lithography extensively in toy train production. It manufactured a sturdy array of models in both O gauge and Wide gauge, which was the same as Lionel Standard. Ives, however, never used the term "Standard" because Lionel was considered its main competitor.

Harry Ives, the son of the founder, was in charge when the train line was introduced. Strong evidence indicates he was not as shrewd as J. Lionel Cowen. The Ives and Lionel lines were roughly equivalent in quality and price. To compete, Ives went a step further than Lionel by offering little extras, such as a liberal trade-in policy and free factory service "for life." Although these gestures built goodwill, they cut deeply into the profit margin. Ives' insistence on never cheapening his products reduced profits even more.

Ives went bankrupt in 1928. The train interests were acquired by a coalition that included Lionel and American Flyer, and the two firms jointly produced Ives merchandise for the next two years. Then Lionel bought out Flyer's share and moved Ives production to the Lionel plant in Irvington, New Jersey. Cowen turned the Ives line into a new low-priced Lionel line. After two more years, he discontinued the Lionel-Ives trains and the Ives name disappeared from the marketplace.

American Flyer. Chicago hardware manufacturer W. O. Coleman and mechanical toy maker William Hafner entered into partnership in 1907 to produce an inexpensive line of clockwork trains under the trade name American Flyer. They experimented with the use of lithography in the low-price end of the market.

Hafner left the company in 1914 to establish his own windup train business. The first American Flyer electrics appeared shortly thereafter. Starting in O gauge, Flyer later joined Lionel and Ives in Wide gauge production. (Coleman also refused to use the term "Standard.") Although the company offered trains at all price levels, it was saddled with an economy

This inexpensive American Flyer O gauge electric train set was kind to Depression-era toy budgets.

This Joy Line electric train from the early 1930s was the forerunner of the toy train line marketed by Louis Marx & Co. The power station accessory houses the set's transformer.

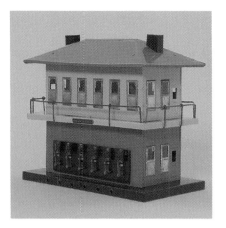

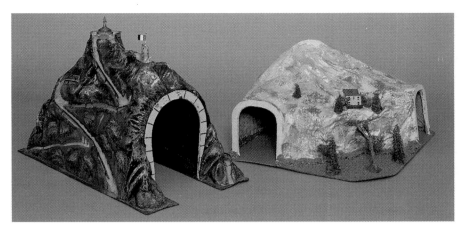

This American Flyer Wide gauge switch tower from the early 1930s was actually very functional. Young engineers could control their trains by using the six knife switches that were mounted on its side.

Tunnels surely are the most popular toy train accessories of all time. Many early ones were painted by hand, including these two: a Märklin tunnel from about 1910 (left) and a Lionel from the 1930s (right).

line image, which put it at a competitive disadvantage.

In 1938 A. C. Gilbert, who had grown famous producing Erector Sets and Mysto-Magic Kits as well as home appliances, bought American Flyer and moved it to his headquarters in New Haven, Connecticut. There he manufactured both O and HO gauge trains until World War II material shortages halted all nonessential production.

Introduced in 1946, the American Flyer S gauge line garnered a loyal following but could not compete effectively with giant Lionel. These ³⁄₁₆-inch scale models were attractive, well-made, and reliable performers, but they were incompatible with the more prevalent O gauge trains. Gilbert's attempt to turn the toy train industry in his direction failed. After almost 30 years of frustration under Gilbert, the company went out of business. Rights to the American Flyer name were acquired by Lionel in 1966.

In 1979 Lionel/Fundimensions reinstituted American Flyer S gauge as a supplement to its regular O gauge business. A limited line of these trains is still being produced by Lionel.

So, by the mid-1960s, Lionel had swallowed up two of its major competitors, American Flyer and Ives. It was not healthy enough then, however, to go after the one remaining, Louis Marx; the fickle toy market had shifted so drastically that the Lionel Corporation's own days as a toy train manufacturer were numbered.

SOME THAT CAME LATER

Marx. Although a major toy maker, Marx was a latecomer to the train business. In the early 1930s, toy salesman Louis Marx obtained an interest in a Pennsylvania company that manufactured, among other things, cheap mechanical trains under the Joy Line brand. His own train line evolved from it and became a small yet notable part of the Marx empire.

With inexpensive, durable windup and electric trains, Marx had a corner on the low end of the market almost immediately. His no-frills locomotives retailed for a dollar, his cars for a dime. Consumers took to the idea that they could put together their own sets à la carte, depending upon what they liked and how much they could afford to spend.

This beautiful O scale, three-rail model of the famed Milwaukee Road Hiawatha (produced by MTH Electric Trains) is a good example of the kinds of products that started becoming available to toy train hobbyists in the early- to mid-1990s.

An exquisitely detailed model of the king of steam locomotives, the Union Pacific Big Boy, comes from Third Rail. This handsome engine is designed to run on O gauge hi-rail layouts.

Marx was the Henry Ford of the train business, at least at the start. His products were reliable and priced within reach of almost everyone. In a real sense, Marx brought the toy train to the masses. Although the original company went out of business in 1975, the train line was revived in the early 1990s. New Marx trains are again available to collectors and operators.

The success of Lionel/Fundimensions in developing a new market for toy trains in the 1970s pointed to an even larger potential among O gauge collectors and operators. A number of smaller, specialized companies soon sprang up. Five of them have grown into significant forces in today's hi-rail market.

K-Line. This is the only company other than Lionel with a full line of toy trains, track, and accessories. It makes attractive, well-proportioned rolling stock and locomotives that run smoothly.

MTH. A newcomer that offers three lines of imported locomotives, cars, and accessories. The Premier line consists of high-quality O scale/gauge models. Rail-King trains are smaller, in the O-27 tradition. Tinplate Traditions pieces are mainly reproductions of Lionel Standard Gauge cars, locomotives, and accessories.

Third Rail. An up-and-coming supplier of full-scale imported brass hi-rail models in a variety of prototypes, it has made "big" locomotives its specialty thus far.

Weaver. This company produces a highly detailed line of brass steam locomotives, plastic diesels, and scale cars suitable for use on scale or hi-rail layouts. The models are available both ways.

Williams. Originally a supplier of restoration parts, it soon began reproducing scarce toy train classics. Its line of highly detailed locomotives and colorful passenger cars has met with wide acceptance among collectors and operators alike.

TOY TRAINS TODAY: COLLECTORS AND OPERATORS

Today's beginning train enthusiast is in a great position. Interest in the hobby has never been higher. New technologies and electronic miniaturization allow today's model trains to perform feats undreamed of a few years ago. Product quality is excellent, amid a wide variety of choices. Helpful books and magazines are abundant, providing guidance in building an operating layout, starting a train collection, or both. A

Perhaps Lionel's signature locomotive is the EMD F3. First produced in the late 1940s in Santa Fe and New York Central liveries, the classic "covered wagon" shell has been decorated in dozens of road names and has been cataloged almost continuously to the present day.

thriving market in new and used trains and accessories has brought the hobby to the attention of a broad and diverse population nationwide.

What is so appealing about model trains? The answers are many. The pleasures can be personal, but generalizations are possible. For clarity, let's separate the collecting aspects from the operating ones, even though such a division may not exist.

The fulfillment gained from collecting trains is similar to that in other collecting hobbies. There is the thrill of the hunt. Then there is the satisfaction of completing some phase or filling in a gap. For many enthusiasts, an inherent pride in ownership comes with sharing an interesting collection with friends and colleagues. Underneath it all lies an appreciation of the art, science, and technology that went into these artifacts and what they represent in popular culture.

On the building and operating side, there is the rush of raw creative energy that comes in planning and constructing a fine layout, the kind of hands-on activity that many people lack in their daily routines. Solving operating problems as they arise, shifting cars in the yard, making up trains and running them according to schedule can be just as challenging as a game of chess. The ultimate reward is undoubtedly the sense of absolute power that comes from controlling a miniature world, built to your own specifications. It's more than merely fun.

To top it all, there is the slaying of the old "silk purse–sow's ear" maxim. Few other hobbies provide so many opportunities to make something beautiful and worthwhile out of practically nothing. Most model railroad landscapes are laid upon beds of discarded newspapers. Buildings can be fabricated from old shoe boxes or shirt cardboard. With a little time and effort, beat-up locomotives and cars can be recycled into good-looking, functional rolling stock. Through careful and loving restoration, even treasured antique pieces can have the ravages of time reversed and, like the phoenix, rise from the ashes to live once more.

Age and gender lines are far less distinct than they once were. For more than half a century, trains were marketed as a masculine hobby, bridging generations and bonding fathers and sons in lifetime partnerships. Today, the hobby works as well with fathers and daughters, even husbands and wives. Instead of proceeding upward from the children to the parents, the perspective has also changed. According to the most successful contemporary examples, the hobby is family oriented yet adult centered.

The schism between scale and toy trains is narrowing as the emphasis shifts on both sides. Toy trains are becoming more realistic, evolving from the bizarre and gaudy childhood playthings they once were. On the other hand, many scale models are being packaged "ready-to-run," eliminating the model maker's mystique and minimizing the omnipresent need for manual dexterity and technical expertise. The compromises are healthy on a level that makes today's trains, whether toy or scale, appealing and available to anyone who would like to enter the hobby.

But before we get carried away by the spirit of model railroad brotherhood and lost forever in the euphoria of some domestic version of world reconciliation, we should not lose sight of which one came first.

It was the toy train!

Here is why the terms "gauge" and "scale" should not be used interchangeably. Both of these Lionel locomotives were designed and built to run on O gauge track. Neither is in strictly ¼-inch scale, although the Reading Lines T-1 on the right is closer than the 1681.

THE DIFFERENCE BETWEEN GAUGE AND SCALE

THE TERMS "gauge" and "scale" have often been used interchangeably, thereby misleading and confusing many beginning model train hobbyists. Technically, gauge refers only to the distance between the track running rails, while scale is a proportion, a comparative ratio of a model's measurements to the dimensions of the full-size prototype.

For example, O gauge track has a distance of 1.25" (31.8 mm) between the running rails. This is a fairly universal standard. O scale is a 1:48 proportion, which means 1" on the model's surface represents 48" on the prototype. Expressed another way, ¼ inch equals 1 foot. A model of this size is said to be in "¼" scale," which is appropriate for O gauge track.

Therefore, an exact O scale model of an 80-foot passenger car would be 20 inches long. The trains built and operated by scale model railroaders adhere strictly to these standards of proportion. Toy trains fudge them a bit, however. Lionel's extruded aluminum passenger cars, the longest the company ever manufactured for O gauge track, measure only 16 inches in length. Although they may fall short of being accurate scale models, they look right in their own context and appear massive when compared to smaller Lionel coaches.

The liberties taken with the proportions, particularly length, of toy trains have good reason. Scale length rolling stock requires a wide turning radius. Toy trains must function in small spaces, so it is necessary to reduce their dimensions.

This compressing must be done with an artistic eye to retain the illusion of correct proportions. The trains might not be in scale, but they should appear to be. This is particularly important with locomotives. Except for the famous full-scale Hudsons, most Lionel engines have been shrunk considerably. Yet they all run on the same O gauge track, and they look right doing it. Lionel's engineering staff has always been highly skilled at this technique.

Because O gauge is by far the most prevalent in the toy train world, the emphasis of this book is put on it. For the sake of comparison, however, here is a rundown of all the popular gauges in descending order of size.

STANDARD GAUGE

Standard gauge track has a distance of 2.26" between running rails. There probably never was an official Standard scale because the peak popularity of this gauge predated widespread interest in scale model railroading. It was the premier toy train gauge from World War I through the early 1930s.

Lionel coined the term Standard gauge and claimed the exclusive rights to its use. Both American

Flyer and Ives also manufactured trains with this track configuration, but referred to them as Wide gauge. By the turn of the 1940s, Standard gauge toy trains had all but vanished from the scene.

A few independent manufacturers began producing new and original Standard gauge items for collectors as early as the 1970s, but it was not until the classic Lionel trains were reproduced in the middle 1980s that significant interest in this gauge revived.

G GAUGE

The term G gauge is used to describe a variety of popular large scale trains with widely differing proportions. Technically it is incorrect. The track, the only thing that most of these trains have in common, is identical to the old No. One gauge, having 1.77″ between the running rails. Number One scale has a proportion of 1:32 or .37″ to the foot. European train makers have used it for years.

G scale is a 1:22.6 proportion, or .63″ to the foot. On that basis, G gauge track would require 2.6″ between the rails. When Lehmann Patentwerk, a German firm, began manufacturing its LGB brand of large scale trains in the late 1960s, its engineers followed European narrow gauge prototypes. As a result, they gave its models a whimsical look—short, fat, and top-heavy—that many people found appealing. These LGB trains were scale models with excellent detail, but they looked more toylike than anything else on the market. Of course G scale narrow gauge track was about the same as the No. One gauge track, which was already available.

Over the last 20 years, half a dozen other manufacturers have entered the large scale train field, all using the same track gauge. Scales range from 1:20 to 1:32, with steps in between at 1:22.6, 1:24, and 1:29.

O GAUGE

O scale is a 1:48 proportion, or ¼ inch to the foot. O gauge track measures 1.26″ between running rails. This is the most popular toy train gauge by far. The tinplate track is commonly found in two basic profiles, regular O gauge and O-27, and at least five different curvatures.

Regular O gauge Lionel track has a railhead height of 1¹⁄₁₆″ and a circle diameter of 31″. Wider radius O-72 is of the same profile, but with a 72″ diameter.

Track of the second profile, known as O-27, is formed from lighter-weight steel and has a railhead height of ⁷⁄₁₆″. A circle has a 27″ diameter. Two wider-radius versions of this track are also available from Lionel, O-42 and O-64.

The two profiles were not designed to be mixed. They can be used together on the same layout, however, if the O-27 track is shimmed by ¼″ and the holes in the tubular rails are enlarged to accept regular O gauge pins.

Generally, most O gauge equipment, except for the largest locomotives and passenger cars, will operate satisfactorily on O-27 track. And, with the exception of

Size comparisons of the various popular toy train gauges. Looking from left to right, you can see G, Standard, O, S, and HO gauges.

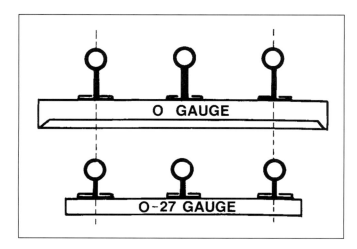

Lionel O and O-27 gauge track profiles.

Lionel four-wheel-drive steamers made before 1948 and some early Marx units, most O-27 trains will work on regular O gauge track.

Several independent manufacturers also produce O gauge tinplate track in different curvatures, but in profiles similar to Lionel.

S GAUGE

S scale is a proportion of 1:64, or ³⁄₁₆ inch to the foot. S gauge track measures .87″ between the running rails. This scale became popular after World War II, when The A.C. Gilbert Co. converted its entire American Flyer train line from O to S scale, which was considered by many to be an excellent com-

promise, falling approximately halfway between O at 1:48 and HO at 1:87.

HO GAUGE

This designation came from England more than 65 years ago and originally was meant to convey the idea that the scale was Half of O. (Close, but no crumpets!) The proportion is 1:87, or 3.6 millimeters to the foot. Track measures .66 inch (16.6 mm) between the running rails.

HO has been the overwhelming choice among scale model railroaders for a long time. The story of HO toy trains is different. Perhaps because of their size they could not withstand abuse from children as well as could larger trains. In spite of excellent marketing and competitive pricing, HO toy train sets never really caught on. Some are still available, but they represent a small percentage of toy train sales.

N, Z, AND OTHER GAUGES

N scale is a proportion of 1:160, or .07″ to the foot. N gauge is .36″ (9 mm) between the rails. This always has been a scale model railroader's size. The trains were rarely sold as toys.

Over the years, several other gauges have achieved popularity for a while and then vanished. For example, OO (1:76) showed some promise in the late 1930s. TT (1:120) came and went in the 1950s.

Z (1:220) arrived from Germany a few years ago, but has not set this part of the world on fire. It probably never will, except among people with exceptionally keen eyesight, and those who operate flea circuses!

DETERMINING VALUE AND PRICE

HOW MUCH IS a train worth? That depends upon the train and the buyer. Intrinsically, little. If the human body is composed of $1.98 worth of chemicals, the few ounces of metal and plastic in any train can't amount to much. Value, that elusive intangible, exists only in the mind of the buyer. Therefore, a train is worth exactly what someone is willing to pay for it, no more and no less.

All the price and value guides that have inundated the market with hype and folklore for more than two decades are merely that—guides, rules of thumb at best. Although they might give some indication of relative desirability, the prices quoted usually bear only faint resemblance to those in the real world. The guides are useful mainly because they catalog the output of the various train manufacturers in an organized way.

Age and rarity mean little. Just because a piece is old or rare does not necessarily indicate a high price tag. Some of the oldest trains gather dust on dealers' shelves for years because nobody is interested in them at any price. There are no collectors, no market. Rarity can also be a hindrance. Sometimes a train can be so rare that few collectors know about it. That makes it more a curiosity than a collectible. It will have limited appeal and a narrow market because mainstream collector interest is elsewhere.

Oddly enough, the trains that command the highest prices are not particularly old or scarce. Instead they have qualities or characteristics that capture the imaginations of many collectors, thereby making them desirable and sought-after items. These are often top-of-the-line sets that originally were priced out of reach of many families and today represent belated childhood wish-fulfillment. When the dreams of youth come true in adulthood, they tend to cost a lot more. Essentially, this is what creates the demand that affects the supply and determines the market price.

Guides with current prices of toy trains are readily available.

THE NOSTALGIA MARKET DEMAND AND PRICE BEHAVIOR

Because having a child legitimizes the natural urge in adults to play with toys, many people are reacquainted with toy trains when their kids reach train age. After buying the initial set for their offspring, parents often begin searching for toy railroad relics from their own childhood to add to the fun. This is known as the "nostalgia market," a lucrative one that all used train dealers nurture and cherish.

There is a fairly stable and predictable demographic profile for these new entrants into the hobby. They all have at least one young child, probably between six and ten years of age. They are fairly affluent and range in age from 30 to 45. The nostalgia market usually corresponds to a time frame or period of train production between 20 and 35 years prior to the date of entry, when the newcomers were themselves boys with trains. This nostalgia market dictates the type and the era of train products that will show the highest price growth rate at any given time.

The infusion of this new blood has a sharp inflationary impact upon prices because people tend to spend more when getting started than they do later. They feel the need to acquire basic items quickly; because they are not familiar with current market prices, they often pay more than necessary for them. And with more people bidding in the market, demand stays high.

As this 20- to 35-year lag created by the nostalgia market advances through time, prices on the leading edge jump quickly and continue to rise for several years. On the trailing edge, they level off and remain constant for a while. Many eventually decline. At that point, supply and demand become tempered by other factors. Historically, this pattern has held for as long as statistical information on the train collecting hobby has been available.

CONDITION AND PRICE

A major consideration in determining price is the condition of the train. Years ago, the Train Collectors Association (TCA), the largest and oldest organization of toy train collectors, devised criteria for evaluating the condition of used trains. Although many collectors have their own methods and the TCA criteria are more often honored in the breach, they do provide a logical and workable set of standards:

• MINT: Brand new, absolutely unmarred; all original and unused
• LIKE NEW: Free of any blemishes, nicks, or scratches; original condition throughout; very little sign of use
• EXCELLENT: Minute nicks or scratches; no dents or rust
• VERY GOOD: A few scratches; exceptionally clean; no dents or rust
• GOOD: Scratches, small dents, dirty
• FAIR: Well scratched, chipped, dented, rusted or warped
• POOR: Beat-up, junk condition; some usable parts

Three identical Lionel tank cars in various conditions. Front: According to TCA standards, this car would probably be graded between "Like New" and "Excellent." Middle: This model would fall in the "Good" to "Very Good" range because it lacks its original luster and has nicks and scratches as well as a bit of rust on the frame. Rear: This car would be judged "Fair" or even "Poor" because of the large area of missing paint and significant amounts of rust on its frame and trucks.

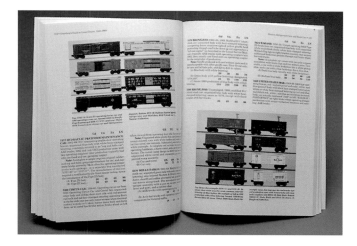

Paging through any of the colorful price and reference guides can be great fun and very informative. In fact, it can be a nostalgic trip in itself.

Be aware that the TCA standards apply mainly to the condition of the original finish, regardless of whether the train works. Operation is unimportant to many collectors, as long as the paint is good and all the parts are there. Restored or repainted trains are judged on a different basis.

Some price guides use the TCA standards of condition, and some do not. Unfortunately, this lack of consistency adds to the confusion and misunderstanding that can occur when people are trying to determine a fair price for a particular item.

Let's use an example to show how condition can affect price. We will use the TCA criteria on a model in Like New condition, valued at $100. The same item in Excellent condition might be expected to bring between $70 and $80. At Very Good, the price range would be about $50 to $60. In Good condition, the piece might sell for $30 to $40. Trains in Fair or Poor condition are not highly regarded by collectors, except for use as temporary hole fillers or as sources of original parts. As such, the same model might go for $10 to $20.

Trains in Mint condition, those truly unused and unmarred, are extremely hard to find; therefore, they are prized by collectors. Our $100 example could easily sell for between $125 and $150. If it is in the original box, add at least 25 percent more. Collectors are big on boxed items. Complete boxed sets of almost any age are in high demand and command premium prices.

Regardless of the language they may use in describing condition, most of the value and price guides reflect this kind of graduated price scale. The problem with the use of these handy guides is that few people pay attention to the prices listed for the lesser grades. Their eyes catch the quotations in the Like New or Excellent column and go no farther.

TRAIN PRICING IN THE FUTURE

In the past, the influx of nostalgia entrants with strong emotional ties to their own childhood toys caused price increases among used trains of a certain age. Now the handwriting is on the wall. As I mentioned, the toy train industry foundered in the 1960s. Product quality was at an all-time low. Trains were no longer marketed as the "in" gifts from parent to child. Kids themselves preferred robots, rockets, and road-racing to railroading.

The trains produced after the mid-1970s were aimed at a different group of buyers. So, when parents of the future look back for a nostalgic tie with their own youth in the special toys they buy for their children, will they look at a train set? Probably not. The nostalgia market will vanish.

This change does not spell doom for the toy train hobby. There undoubtedly will be new recruits in the future, because the hobby is healthy. Entry, however, will be based upon something other than the tug of childhood nostalgia. People will find new reasons to become interested.

The train fans of the future will probably be more involved with operation in general and the construction of hi-rail layouts. They will certainly be more aware of quality and technology. Many will view vintage toy trains as historical artifacts of American popular culture. Some will specialize in restoring old pieces to their original condition. Others will look for the friendly competition and comradeship that already exists among serious hobbyists. The kinship with the scale model railroading community will become closer as the two groups explore each other's domains.

The number of new entrants each year will level off from the record highs of the past decade. That means prices, particularly for common, used items in less-than-pristine condition, also will level off and probably fall as the demand lessens. With the emotional nostalgia component missing, the prices of toy trains will reflect a more realistic assessment of their quality, performance, and intrinsic worth. The dizzying ride on the escalator to the stars will come to an end.

Meanwhile, the prices of new products will have to be brought within the reach of the less wealthy, particularly the middle class. Whether this change actually occurs will be up to the manufacturers. In the past, they have been creating new collectibles each year, priced on the basis of what the traffic could be made to bear. In the long run, bringing down prices should broaden the base and increase the volume of sales.

With the decline of the nostalgia elements during the past few years, collector emphasis has shifted toward the newer, scale-like products marketed by Lionel, MTH, K-Line, Weaver, Third Rail, Williams, and the like. This obviously follows the trend toward construction of more realistic hi-rail layouts by the ever-increasing number of hobbyists who consider

DEMOGRAPHIC PROFILE

According to the most recent survey conducted by *Classic Toy Trains,* the "typical" toy train hobbyist is:

• A 52-year-old married man with children. He enjoyed toy trains in his childhood and became involved with them again about 20 years ago. He shares his interest with at least one relative or friend.

• He is enthusiastic about the hobby. He reads related books and magazines and may even use his computer to help him enjoy it. His interest has not diminished in the past year; in fact, it may have grown.

• His major focus is on the Lionel O gauge trains manufactured between 1945 and the present. He considers himself to be both a collector and an operator of those trains.

• His home layout contains approximately 213 square feet and is either of traditional design or combines traditional and hi-rail elements.

• His annual income is approximately $73,500, and he spends about $1,500 on toy trains and related merchandise.

themselves to be both collectors and operators (almost 70 percent, according to the latest reader survey conducted by *Classic Toy Trains* magazine).

This shift could well be the wave of the future. Highly detailed, reliable, ready-to-run locomotives and cars in the O gauge, three-rail format will take their place alongside traditional Lionel rolling stock on collectors' shelves and layouts across America. Whether these new products will ever become sought-

after collectibles in the sense of the older Lionel trains remains to be seen.

TOY TRAINS AS INVESTMENTS

Speculators who did not see or care about the big picture or the long run jumped headlong into the nostalgia-driven toy train market of the 1980s, when prices of toy trains showed their sharpest upward spiral ever. Some smart traders doubled their money in a short

CORRELATIONS BETWEEN TRAIN COLLECTING EMPHASIS AND THE NOSTALGIA MARKET, 1955–1995

Year	Nostalgia market frame of years	Median nostalgia market year	Standard gauge	Prewar O gauge	Postwar O gauge	S gauge	Toy HO gauge	Other favorite toys*
1955	1920–1935	(1927)	A					
1960	1925–1940	(1932)	A	B				
1965	1930–1945	(1937)	A	A				
1970	1935–1950	(1942)	B	A				
1975	1940–1955	(1947)	B	A	B	B		
1980	1945–1960	(1952)		B	A	A		
1985	1950–1965	(1957)		B	A	A	B	
1990	1955–1970	(1962)			A	A	A	B
1995	1960–1975	(1967)			B	B	B	A
(2000?)	1965–1980	(1972)			B			A

A = Strong emphasis
B = Transitional (weaker) emphasis
(*) Rockets, robots, road racing, video games, computers, etc.
Note: No data available before the mid-1950s

time. Overall, toy trains performed better than stocks and bonds. For the first time, they were considered to be a serious investment. This generated a lot of publicity and media attention.

In the ensuing frenzy, many people with visions of dollar signs dancing in their heads entered the toy train market, thereby polluting it seriously. Most of them ended up disappointed. As with all kinds of commodity trading, the trick is in knowing what to buy and when to sell. For every smart winner there has to be at least one dumb loser. A seller isn't really a seller until he can find a buyer. This kind of dealing is not for the inexperienced and uninitiated, so don't trade your IRAs for trains just yet.

As pure investments, some of the better Lionel sets produced in the late 1970s and early 1980s appreciated well. One that retailed for $225 then brought $750 in the early 1990s. Another went up from $400 to about $1,000 in the same period. However, these two isolated examples were desirable trains with relatively low prices going in.

Most sets did not fare as well, particularly in more recent times. As the number of speculators in the marketplace increased, so did the initial retail prices. This effectively froze out a large number of smaller would-be investors. Not many of us can afford to pay $1,500 or $2,000 for a train and then sit on it for years in the hope that it will increase in value faster than the rate of inflation. Remember, you can't run these trains—they have to remain boxed to be considered mint.

This is not to say that bargains can't still be found or that you should abandon all hopes of using your trains as a form of investment. Still, I think you'll have a much healthier outlook if you follow this advice: If you are turned on by some of the newer trains and just have to add them to your collection or layout, great. Buy and enjoy! Just don't expect to sell them at a profit down the road, too. Those days may well be over.

An array of toy train auction literature. Note the announcement from Christie's, the well-known auction house; it signals the entry of vintage toy trains into the big-time antique world.

BUYING, SELLING, AND TRADING TRAINS

IN SPITE of what you may think, chances are good that eventually you will be buying, selling, and trading toy trains. It just seems to work out that way, particularly if you are interested in the more common and plentiful varieties of trains. Most collectors upgrade their collections as they find items in better condition. Often used trains are found in sets or lots or boxes containing duplicate or uninteresting pieces along with the treasures. Although the temptation to keep everything is great at first, space and other limitations soon dictate otherwise. As collectors become more selective and specialized, their collections are weeded and thinned out, with the surplus being sold or traded off. Many hobbyists find that selling and trading can be just as much fun as buying.

Next to *caveat emptor,* "let the buyer beware," the best advice for new train collectors would be "do your homework." Research the field. Read whatever you can find on the subject—books, hobby magazines, and the like. Shop around. Talk to other collectors. Most are helpful and willing to share stories and information. If

possible, find an experienced friend to serve as a mentor, particularly if your interests include trains no longer in production. Even if you collect only the newer trains, a knowledgeable friend may steer you toward the dealers with the best prices.

TRACKING DOWN OLD TRAINS

"Gold is where you find it," was a popular expression among prospectors during the California gold rush of 1849. This saying applies today to the search for old toy trains. Some are almost as valuable. Although the trains are more plentiful and easier to find than gold, you have to know how and where to look for them.

Consider this. During the peak years, annual toy train production numbered in the millions of units. One of every three or four American households with boys over a certain age had a toy train in it at one time. Many of those trains are still there, gathering dust in the attic or rust in the basement, just waiting to be rediscovered.

The following seven suggested sources of old toy trains are tried and true. They are presented as starting points as you enter this fascinating and engrossing hobby.

Private homes, garage sales, estate sales. We know of one collector who canvassed door-to-door, much like a brush salesman or census taker, searching for trains. He was successful, too, particularly in the older, more stable neighborhoods. Of course, he was retired and had the time.

Classified ads in newspapers and magazines. Start with your local paper; sometimes the "Miscellaneous—For Sale" columns will specify trains. Also look under "T" for trains, and "E" for electric trains. You'll soon get the hang of it. Don't miss the weekend listings for rummage and garage sales. Estate sales are particularly good these days. Better yet, place your own ad in the "Wanted to Buy" section. It's amazing what still turns up using this simple and direct method, and the whole process is exciting. First, there's the anticipation. Then, the thrill of the hunt, the joy of discovery, and the flush of victory as you bag your prize and carry it home.

Usually trains acquired from their original owners will not have been altered to make them more appealing or marketable. For this reason alone, buying trains from private individuals can be an excellent way to build your collection, particularly if you're a beginner.

But don't necessarily expect bargains. In recent years, many people have become aware of the inflated prices paid for old trains. In fact, popular mythology abounds at the grass roots level that all toy trains are valuable antiques that command large dollars. Don't become discouraged, embarrassed, insulted, or indignant when you run into this. It goes with the territory, a hazard common to all collecting hobbies during their growth stages. Try to be honest and fair. If a reasonable offer elicits an unreasonable response, walk away.

Mail order. As the train collecting hobby grew and spread into less densely populated areas, mail-order train buying became practical. Today, most dealers send lists periodically to their regular customers. Some even have websites on the Internet. Hobby magazines feature classified sections and display ads full of mail-order merchandise. Collecting organizations circulate flyers that often contain little more than items offered for sale or trade by their membership. Some large suppliers publish catalogs.

Buying trains through the mail can be efficient, but pitfalls loom. If you know the seller, either personally or by reputation, fine. If not, be careful. When the transaction is not face-to-face, misunderstandings regarding grading standards or flaws overlooked by the seller are common. Before you buy anything, make sure you can return the merchandise if you aren't satisfied. Reputable dealers will allow it. Collecting organizations insist on it.

Hobby shops. These establishments are among the best and safest sources. Like most retailers, they want repeat business. So they often give guarantees, allow trade-ins, take returns, accept credit cards, provide layaways and service after the sale. Expect to pay extra for these amenities. Proprietors of such shops are often wonderful sources of information and hobby folklore. They come highly recommended, particularly for beginners.

Swap meets and train shows. Meets and shows are great fun in what is almost a carnival atmosphere. Trains of all sizes and ages piled high on the tables. Buyers and sellers everywhere. These events are often good sources of bargains, particularly if you're handy at fixing things. They range in scope from the extravaganzas put on once or twice a year by national collecting associations down to the small, local events held at fraternal organizations, fire stations, and bowling alleys.

Swap meets and train shows offer a chance to see the merchandise, touch and test it, ask questions, and haggle over prices. Be sure you know exactly what you are looking for, because what you see is what you get. Don't expect the seller to refund your money because you changed your mind or made a mistake; he may not even be there when you return.

You can always find toy trains for sale in the classified advertising sections of newspapers and magazines. These samples come from the *Milwaukee Journal-Sentinel*, *Classic Toy Trains*, and *Model Railroader*.

Sommerfeld's Trains in Butler, Wisconsin, deals exclusively in trains. Here, as in other well-stocked hobby stores, customers find vintage and new toy trains as well as scale models, track, scenicking materials, and more. Repairs are expertly done, and advice is freely dispensed.

Auctions. These can be good, sometimes. You may even get lucky on a price, but don't count on it. Auctioneers rarely know what a train may actually be worth, but their natural tendency is to start the bidding on the high side. No rules apply. "Old" or "cute" often equates with an elevated opening estimate. Be prepared to compete with high rollers and shills. Bidding at an auction can be an object lesson in compulsive behavior and a short course in mob psychology.

Antique shops. Experience has taught me that these usually are a poor choice. Most are operated by "experts" on everything in the store who have their secret systems of determining prices. Few items have tags. One may infer, therefore, that prices are made up on a case-by-case basis, depending upon what the proprietor thinks a customer is willing to pay.

But antique dealers aren't really selling merchandise. They are peddlers of dreams, fantasies, nostalgic remembrances of better days in a golden past. How can such intangibles be priced? It is best to leave such places before you inhale too much of the ambience.

Trades with other collectors. These one-on-one transactions are usually straightforward and can be rewarding. The problem is finding someone who has what you want and is willing to trade it for what you have. Often such trading deteriorates into simple buying and selling.

INS AND OUTS OF BUYING TRAINS AT SHOWS AND SWAP MEETS

While geared to the basic circumstances of swap meets, these guidelines will serve the uninitiated train buyer in other places and situations as well. Although they resemble flea markets and gypsy camps on the surface, these train events usually have rules govern-

ing them. Most are sponsored by groups or organizations that have a vested interest in promoting the hobby, and they are concerned about scam artists and fly-by-nighters bilking their customer-guests. While the organizations don't guarantee purchases made under their auspices, most want to know about unresolved disputes and misunderstandings. Some may impose sanctions against unsatisfactory member-dealers. Others simply refuse table space to repeat offenders. These mechanisms only apply in extreme cases, so check the ground rules in advance.

While *caveat emptor* is the accepted swap meet credo, most regular dealers are fairly honest, or at least try to be fair. Many are there primarily because they enjoy the hobby, too. Personal attention and repeat business from regular customers are their lifeblood. In a sense, they are throwbacks to an era before there were superstores, plastic wrap, and computerized customer service. In a world of homogenized and conglomerated retailing, these independent, weekend capitalists stand out. Perhaps that's why they are considered "fair game" by so many of their shopkeeper competitors and officious consumers, who forever snipe at them and foster the notion that swap meet dealers are categorically suspect, and, if not genetically inferior, at least below the societal norm—a bit shady or shifty. In the long run, such disparagement only serves to make the game more interesting. Sometimes, though, the dealers become wary and defensive.

"Look lady, this isn't Marshall Field's!" Words overheard at a recent meet from a dealer who is normally calm and friendly. Having been chiseled to the bone, stiffed with bad checks, stung holding merchandise "until later," shoplifted, haggled, and heckled once too

Hot deals on a cold day at the Great American Train Show, which is held each month at the DuPage County Fairgrounds in Wheaton, Illinois.

often, even the most optimistic can become impatient or cynical. So don't expect trade-ins, unlimited return privileges, layaways, or gift wrap. Few dealers are equipped to handle credit card purchases. And don't be surprised or hurt if they refuse to take your check, no matter how many forms of identification you present. It isn't you, it's the protocol, the first rule of the swap meet game: CASH AND CARRY.

What you see is what you get. All swap meet merchandise is sold as-is. While flaws and malfunctions should be noted, don't assume anything. Ask! Guarantees are rarely given, not even 5 minutes or 50 feet. Your best assurance is to buy from a dealer who has a good reputation or attends the meets regularly. That way, if you have a problem, you'll know where to find him next time. Ask the people who are sponsoring the meet if the dealer is a regular. Some dealers display business cards. Take one. If there are conditions regarding the sale, have the dealer note them on the back of the card or on a sheet of paper. Most will comply gladly. If they refuse, walk away.

Look over the merchandise carefully. Note the flaws. Ask questions about it before you start negotiating. Is it all original? Does it work? Ask to take it to the test track so you can check the performance. No one will be offended; that is accepted practice. Some dealers require a security deposit on merchandise removed from the table. That is also accepted practice, particularly at crowded meets where the test track is near the door. Nothing personal. Remember two things at this point: First, "I don't know" in response to "Does it work?" usually means it doesn't! Second, "Would you take $___?" is not a rhetorical question; it's an offer to buy.

That brings us to the exciting part, the negotiation. Some dealers hold firmly to their ticket prices, considering them to be fair appraisals of market value. Others, who believe that dickering is part of the process of selling, will price their merchandise accordingly, building in an extra margin so they can discount it if necessary. (If you've ever bought a used car, you know the drill.) The bottom line will probably be the same. A third group doesn't believe in ticket prices at all and will give you oral quotes if you ask. Give these dealers a wide berth unless you really know what you are doing. Even then, move cautiously.

The key to successful bargaining is in making a reasonable offer. Chiseling 10 to 15 percent from the ticket price in good-faith negotiation will probably be acceptable to most dealers. Some will consider larger discounts, but that is hard to predict. Package deals are good. Volume buying will often get you a few more total percentage points.

You can try making a ridiculous offer—and you may be successful—but don't count on it. Chances are, once you have made such an offer you will have lost your edge in negotiations that follow. It is hard to bargain with someone who is laughing at you. Unless the dealer is new at it or hasn't done his homework, his asking price represents the ballpark amount he feels confident of getting in the current market. Offers that deviate too far from it will not be taken seriously.

The world's greatest toy train swap meet is held twice a year in York, Pennsylvania. Manufacturer, dealer, and hobbyist tables occupy more than a half-dozen large buildings at the York fairgrounds and more than 10,000 Train Collectors Association members attend the two-day meet. Right: Over the years, the York "pre-show" meets, held in a motel ballroom and parking lots, have grown in popularity with TCA members and non-members alike.

A dealer's willingness to negotiate on price can be contingent on many variables. Here's a list of the more common ones:

Price of the item. Bigger-ticket items, those tagged in multiples of a hundred dollars, are usually more open to negotiation and a wider range of offers than the $5 and $10 things. Perhaps this is because above a certain level, prices become abstract and unreal for many people. The concept of $5 is concrete for everyone. Five hundred becomes more nebulous. Five thousand is just so many zeroes on a piece of paper. This probably applies to buyers and sellers alike. The dealer must turn over his higher-priced items to keep his cash flowing.

Length of time the dealer has carried the item. This is hard to find out. Sometimes a dealer will accept almost any offer just to unload what he considers to be dead weight in his inventory, or he'll settle for recouping his investment without a profit. He may even take a loss.

Volume of traffic at the meet. On a slow day, almost anything is possible. Many sellers are on a tight margin and must generate a certain dollar value at each meet to stay in business. Under such circumstances, even ridiculous offers are sometimes accepted. At a well-attended meet where sales are brisk, dealers remain bullish.

Time of day. Little price negotiating takes place during the first hour or two of a meet. (This is when the most desirable items are sold, often at or near asking prices.) As the day wears on, sometimes as early as noon, dealers open up to more serious bargaining. Some even make a practice of dropping prices in the early afternoon. (By this time, the choice merchandise is gone.) If you can wait that long and want to drive a hard bargain, make your offer at about four in the afternoon. A fine time to start is when the dealer is packing up to go home. What is left at that time is considered to be "distressed merchandise." If you can use it, you'll probably be able to buy it at a good price.

Season of the year. In most sections of the country, working (or playing) with trains is a wintertime activity. Long, cold nights and the traditional association of trains and the holiday season are the reasons. The train business flourishes as the leaves begin to fall and peaks toward the end of each year. Dealers consider October through February their prime target months for sales. At that time, both the supply and the price of all train merchandise will be at their high points. Not a good time to hunt for bargains. Generally, dealers find offers harder to refuse in May or June.

One final bit of advice: Don't walk around a swap meet thumbing through your pocket price guide. That's a sure sign you're either ripe for picking or looking for an argument. You lose on both counts. The most vulnerable buyer is a neophyte with a book in his hand. If you absolutely have to look up a price, do it in the rest room—with the door closed!

I like to watch people, particularly when they're having fun. For the past 15 years, I have regularly attended train meets and shows. Although I usually can be found behind a dealer's table, I'm not a big-time seller. And if I don't do a lot of selling, I can't do a lot of buying. So I've had the time and opportunity to take in the action and observe the unforgettable characters on both sides of the tables.

The same types of people can be found at collecting confabs everywhere. You'll find them at the annual or semiannual extravaganzas sponsored by national organizations as well as the local events held in bowling alleys, police stations, and elementary schools.

Here they are, then, a rogue's gallery of 40 such types, evenly split between dealers and customers.

DEALERS (SEEN FROM THE CUSTOMER'S PERSPECTIVE)

Wholesale Herman: Has 14 tables piled high with new merchandise from all the leading manufacturers. His prices undercut the competition, both advertised and unadvertised. He claims to sell everything for "cost." When asked how he can do that and stay in business, he shrugs and explains that he buys below cost.

Dealer Wheeler: Fancies himself to be Wholesale Herman's major competitor and positions his table complex accordingly. Formerly in the gasoline business, he often starts price wars just to get Herman steamed. He says he doesn't care if he loses money on every sale. When asked how he can do that and stay in business, he shrugs and explains that he makes it up in volume.

Parts-Is-Parts Bart: Carrie thousands of items in fishing tackle cases and browser boxes and on pegboard racks. He has parts for obscure trains made 50 years ago, but never seems to have the one you need.

Train Paper Chase: Deals in old railroad timetables, magazines, catalogs, and other train-related paper items, many of which are badly mildewed and crumbling into dust. Customers find his table by sniffing the air or listening for the sound of sneezing.

Bad Meet Pete: Complains constantly about his lack of sales and threatens to quit coming to the meets. He has been carrying around the same overpriced merchandise for the past three years.

Audio Augie: Demonstrates state-of-the-art electronic train sound effects equipment at a decibel level that is always far out of proportion to the scale of the models.

No Price Brice: Never tags anything. The price of an item, one suspects, is determined by how much he thinks the customer is carrying.

Madison Avenue Melvin: Dressed in a suit and tie. Show the slightest interest in something or ask a question, and he launches into a canned 30-second commercial about it.

Spray Wax Max: Everything on his table shines.

Durward the Dumper: Never unpacks, just opens his boxes and pours their contents onto his table.

Vinnie the Intimidator: Has a very high sales volume. He's tall and muscular and stands erect with his chin out and his arms folded. Pick up an item and it's yours. No one has ever dared to make a lower offer.

Hector the Erector: Spends hours constructing elaborate display shelves, back panels, and outriggers, all clamped to his tables. Has to arrive so early to set up everything that he often falls asleep before the meet ends.

Cellophane Blaine: All his stuff is neatly packaged and wrapped in plastic bags. He claims that this keeps items from becoming shopworn; it also hides some of their flaws.

Blue Light Bennie: Spends most of the time at the meet repricing things. He's especially good at this when someone is watching him. His tags always reflect "drastic reductions," "markdowns," and "close-outs." His big scam: He will reduce an item's price every hour until he sells it.

Bad Light Dwight: Sets up in a far corner or unscrews the bulb directly over his table to enhance the condition of his merchandise.

Flea Market Fred: Has a few trains on his table, but really deals in surplus sweat socks, ashtrays, belt buckles, auto parts, and plumbing fixtures.

Oppenheimer the Operator: Always has a layout of some kind chugging and blinking to attract customers to his table.

Whiskey Carton Martin: All his trains are displayed in the compartments of old liquor boxes. This is fine, if you can recognize the piece you're looking for from its end.

Pink Convertible Floyd: Always shows up with his sexy wife or girlfriend. She does the selling while he sits back and handles the money.

Out to Lunch (no last name): Nobody knows him because nobody has ever seen him. He comes early and loads his table with interesting items. Then he disappears for the rest of the meet.

CUSTOMERS (SEEN FROM THE DEALER'S PERSPECTIVE)

Frankie the Finger: He touches everything on the table. He specializes in poking, probing, and spinning wheels. When he picks up an item, he makes sure that his sweaty palms are over the rubber-stamped lettering. His prints wind up on everything at the meet, but he usually leaves empty-handed.

Hal the High-Roller: Carries around a huge wad of bills, which he flashes at every opportunity. However, no one has ever seen him spend more than $2 at a time.

" *VINNIE THE INTIMIDATOR* "

Miller the Scratchbuilder: Religiously attends every meet, trying to find missing parts for a locomotive or carbody that he bought for a bargain price. He's persistent and often is able to piece together a $20 item for $40.

Trader Vic: Carries around a box of battered Scout locomotives and plastic cars that he hopes to parlay into a 773 Hudson.

Boss Hogger: Obsessed with the desire to own every train that was ever made . . . not a copy of each one, but every train.

Henpecked Henry: Attends each and every train show within a 500-mile radius of home. They're his only excuse to get out of the house for a while.

Lowball Lenny and **Would-Ya-Take Jake:** Usually operate as a team, but have been known to do a single number from time to time. They talk loudly to each other, generally casting aspersions about the condition and denigrating the merchandise. Their theory is that the seller may offer them a reduced price just to get them away from the table. Sometimes it even works!

Percy the Purist: Wouldn't think of buying a train unless it had all the original dust on it.

Archie the Antiquarian: Collects only obscure early pieces by Voltamp, Elektoy, and Boucher. He never finds anything, but he's never disappointed either. Probably the only guy who leaves a meet with all the money he came with.

J. Lionel Krylon: This guy has the urge to repaint everything he owns, right over the nicks and rust.

Pocket-Guide Clyde and **Want-List Willie:** Both walk around all day happily thumbing through their little books.

"WANT-LIST WILLIE"

Greg Garious: Always starts a long conversation with four of his friends right in front of your table.

Meanwhile, everyone else has to go around them without ever seeing what you have for sale.

Bruce the Bag Man: Walks around carrying a shopping bag full of stuff. He usually hangs out with Greg Garious and sets his bag on top of your merchandise while they gab.

Last Week Louie: Says he found a train just like the one you have for sale last week, in better condition or cheaper.

Sidestep Sidney: Can be seen with his hands in his pockets, facing the tables, seriously contemplating every last detail on every item. He never looks up or down. He never takes his hands out of his pockets. He walks only sideways.

Know-It-All Paul: Lets you know he's an expert who has seen and handled everything (as he's handling your merchandise). He can tell by the solder joints on your Lionel locomotive how much vino Mario Caruso had for lunch on the day it was made. This is the same guy who will swear up and down that Lionel, Ives, Flyer, or even Marx never produced such a variation. Never! Never! Never!

Arthur the Atheist: Doesn't go to church, so he has to go somewhere on Sunday mornings.

Be-Back Jack: Takes up an hour of your time asking questions and examining your piece from every angle, then says he'll be back later to buy it. His cousin, **Hold-It-for-Me McGee,** uses the same technique. Of course, they're long gone before the meet has ended.

Tony the Test Pilot: Has run more locomotives than Casey Jones. He gets his kicks by taking every engine in sight to the test track. Then he gives his

"BRUCE the BAG MAN"

evaluation of their performance and walks away.

Original Box Wilcox: Never buys anything that isn't in its original, factory-sealed carton, which he never opens. All his boxes are neatly lined up on shelves in his train room. His trains never get dusty that way. He has no need for a layout, but he could use a second-hand X-ray machine. He got a new one last year, but just can't bring himself to take it out of the box.

That's all I could think of. While these 20 dealers and 20 customers are presented as broadly generalized caricatures, anyone who has been to a few train shows will agree that these fellows exist. Look for them the next time you attend a show; you'll be amazed at how many you find.

Two final notes: Try not to laugh too hard when you do run across them. And don't be surprised if one of them is staring back at you in a mirror.

Here is one of the most sought-after items among Lionel postwar collectors. This early run of the O gauge 2338 Milwaukee Road GP7 from 1955 had an orange stripe all around the locomotive. Later runs eliminated it under the cab windows.

PHOTO GALLERY
CLASSIC TRAINS AND ACCESSORIES

THIS IS THE dream and drool section, containing some of the most colorful and sought-after pieces in the world of toy trains. The emphasis is on Lionel products manufactured in the post–World War II era because this represents the bulk of nostalgia and collector interest.

The postwar period also encompasses what for many hobbyists was the golden age of toy trains. That is when postwar technology and manufacturing expertise merged to produce a line of toy trains that had both the look of reality and the charm of toys.

During the years following World War II, consumer demand was at an all-time high. Not only were toy trains the most popular of holiday gifts from parents to children, they had become an integral part of the American Dream.

This is undoubtedly the most popular Lionel locomotive of all time. The O gauge Santa Fe F3 diesel was introduced in 1948 as number 2333 and has often been rerun under different numbers. With its distinctive red warbonnet and yellow trim, this silver beauty is truly a toy train classic.

Lionel's self-propelled motorized units were among the best-liked items in its line in the late 1950s and early '60s. Front (left to right): 60 trolley and 58 rotary snowplow; rear: 50 gang car, 3360 Burro crane, and 68 executive inspection car.

Accessories have always been important contributors to the fun of toy trains. Dave Watson's O gauge layout has many of the popular ones: coal elevator, log loader, diesel fueling station, oil derrick, magnet crane, dispatching tower, and floodlights. There's also a siding for operating milk, cattle, and refrigerator cars.

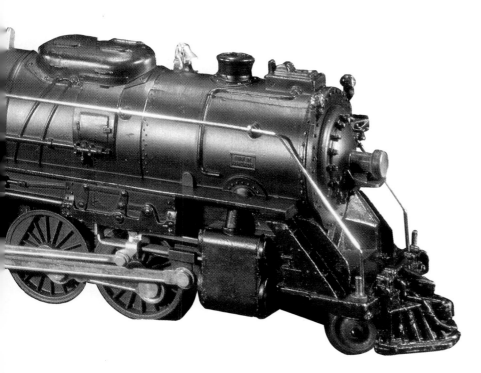

Lionel's large steam power was represented for years by 2-8-4 Berkshires. Produced from 1946 to 1966, the mighty O gauge Berks (numbered 726 and then 736) headed almost every conceivable freight combination in the catalogs.

The 8552-54 Alco A-B-A combination is one of the more colorful O-27 models produced by Lionel/Fundimensions. It was cataloged in 1975.

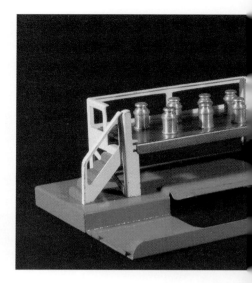

The automatic refrigerated milk car, produced from 1947 to 1955 in this configuration, became the most popular operating car made by Lionel. The little man in his white uniform pops out of the car at the touch of a button and deposits miniature milk cans on the loading platform.

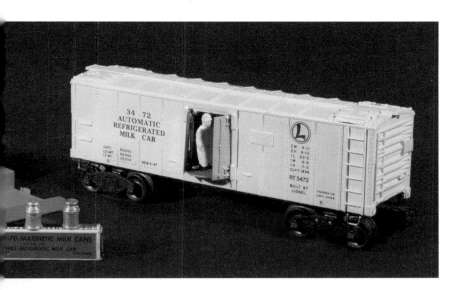

The Girl's Train of 1957 was Lionel's biggest turkey and a charter member in the Marketing Miscalculations Hall of Fame! The catalog boldly stated that the O-27 train came in "fashion-right colors" so it might appeal to daddy's little girl. The train pleased no one, even in that innocent, preliberation era. To recoup their investments, many dealers painted the locomotives black and sold the cars separately. Today, this white (or is it pink?) elephant is a conversation piece much in demand.

Massive diesel motive power, this O gauge model of a Denver & Rio
Grande Western SD50 was equipped with all the latest electronic
devices when offered to hi-railers and modern-era collectors as part
of Lionel's line for 1995.

Starting in 1938, Lionel experimented with marketing a highly
detailed scale model train in the smaller OO gauge. Although the project was not a huge success, the trains produced were miniature mas-
terpieces. Here is the OO Hudson freight set next to its big brother in
O scale. Lionel was in love with Hudsons in those days.

"As the war clouds gathered far across the sea," Louis Marx & Co. came out with a line of O gauge Army Supply Trains. They were made in many variations until metal shortages caused by World War II halted toy train production. (This one looks as if it is coming *back* from the war.)

The A.C. Gilbert Co. cataloged this colorful S gauge Union Pacific passenger set, nicknamed The Pony Express, for only two years, 1959 and 1960. It is highly sought by American Flyer collectors.

These are the almost legendary O gauge Tuscan red Pullman heavyweight passenger cars that Lionel carried over from its prewar line. Named "Madison," "Manhattan," and "Irvington," they are highly prized by collectors, but seldom are found in such good condition because paint adhesion problems often led to massive flaking.

One of the broadest and finest toy train collections belongs to Richard Kughn, the former owner of Lionel. He is one of the few collectors who can truly be called a generalist, as he enjoys toy trains and accessories of all vintages from every manufacturer.

COLLECTORS AND COLLECTIONS

WHO COLLECTS TOY TRAINS and what do they collect? Simple answers could be "anybody" and "everything," but more meaningful generalizations can be drawn. The hobby has a wide appeal that cuts across many strata in our society. Train collectors come from all walks and stations in life. Their range of ages is so broad that it has no real demographic significance.

On economic criteria, the bag is also mixed. Train collectors come from all income levels. There is a heavy concentration among affluent business and professional people. This is based primarily upon observation, since reliable income information is not available.

Although a valid profile of the typical toy train collector would be difficult to construct, one common characteristic is a strong childhood interest in trains. This interest tends to run in families, too, and is passed down from generation to generation.

This family component is significant because the train hobby lends itself to participation by family members without respect to age. Small children find delight in simply watching the trains run. Soon they

learn how to push buttons and make the trains respond. Before long they are sharing in the planning and building of the special "train world" in the basement, attic, or spare room. Toy trains have formed bonds between parents and children for much of the 20th century.

For children who have developed a keen interest and enjoy strong family support, the interest remains strong even during adolescence. The hobby continues despite biological and societal forces that tug in other directions. However, the emphasis often shifts from "playing with toy trains" to the more "realism-oriented" aspects of the hobby. Tinplate layouts evolve into hi-rail ones, with more attention to detail and the total train environment. Some enthusiasts go all the way and convert to scale model railroading.

Other hobbyists lose intensity, become diverted, and drop out, at least for a while. The pressures of completing an education, starting a career, finding a mate, setting up a household, and making ends meet can wreak havoc on any hobby. Trains are relegated to the realm of dreams and futuristic fantasies until these people have children of their own. Then they are likely candidates to return.

In short, some of today's toy train collectors have simply retained their love of trains from youth and continued to build upon it, going through various stages, changes, or specializations along the way. Others have experienced a rekindling of their childhood enthusiasm later in life, when they had children or grandchildren to share in the hobby.

CATEGORIES OF TOY TRAIN COLLECTORS

How many different types of collectors are there? Some observers believe there are as many varieties as there are collectors. They range all the way from broad generalists at one extreme to specialists at the other. Many categories occupy the middle ground, although none of them can be delineated very well.

Even the generalists have some area of focus, such as a particular gauge or era. And the specialists are often involved in more than one specialty. Try as we might, the convenient labels we like to invent won't work here. The train collecting hobby can be tailored to the individual and reflect his changing tastes, needs, and desires.

Unlike the more traditional or established pastimes, you'll find no books of rules or codes of behavior connected with toy train collecting. The hobby is too new. Each collector is free to establish his own criteria and set limitations for himself when and where he chooses. However, since few have the time, money, and facilities to collect everything, collections are usually shaped by practical considerations, such as available space and disposable income.

To further befuddle and complicate attempts at categorization, people change with time. As they learn more and grow, their tastes and goals evolve with them. Some collectors who begin as generalists will eventually specialize. Others who enter the hobby with a precise and narrow focus manage to expand upon it until they appreciate a broader range of possibilities.

As new technologies are developed and new products are introduced, collector emphasis is bound to be affected. The toy train industry is again vital and expanding. Like the trains themselves, most collectors are geared for action; they don't just stand still.

To illustrate the evolutionary nature of the hobby, here are some examples of real people who have been in it for a long time. Their names have been changed to protect the rest of us.

Example 1 (Call him Peter)

Peter had Lionel O gauge trains as a child. More than 35 years ago he began collecting Lionel Standard gauge and top-of-the-line O gauge trains from both the prewar and postwar periods. At one time he was so intensely involved that he bought out a failing Lionel Authorized Service Station/hobby shop for the parts

Specializing in postwar Lionel O gauge is a popular approach to the hobby. Ed Dougherty, a professional golfer, adopted it and owns many of Lionel's Alco diesels, steam engines, and motorized units.

inventory. In the 1980s, he liquidated his collection and turned to the better Lionel/Fundimensions trains. Now he is buying the larger G scale and No. One gauge products as they come out.

Example 2 (Call him Jack)

Jack played with American Flyer S gauge trains as a child. Some 30 years ago, he started to collect Standard gauge trains of all kinds. He sold that collection to go into business for himself. Then he moved into S gauge and at one time had a large collection. He sold it to expand his business. Today he collects only original Lionel and American Flyer postwar boxed sets. He is considering building a hi-rail layout on which to operate contemporary Lionel, MTH, and Williams trains.

Example 3 (Call him Mike)

Mike's childhood interests are unknown. He has been hunting down and buying toy trains of every description since then. He never went through the progressive stages in the hobby. He still has almost everything he has acquired since childhood. It now takes several buildings to house the collection. Although he has no inventory list, he knows exactly what he has—but doesn't necessarily know where it is stored!

Example 4 (Call him Floyd)

Floyd is a qualitative collector. He has owned extensive and valuable collections of many kinds over the years. As his interests changed, he sold most of the pieces from each collection, but retained his favorites. Today his train room looks eclectic and seems to lack any specific theme. Upon careful examination, however, the viewer realizes that Floyd has only the choicest of many different lots.

Example 5 (Call him Al)

Al has been fascinated by toy trains of every variety all of his life. One of the pioneer collectors, he is also one of the world's best "horse traders." He ran newspaper ads for years and regularly visited Goodwill and Salvation Army thrift stores. His extensive, well-organized collection consisted mainly of prewar O and Standard gauge items and was complete in many areas. He liked to run his trains on a large operating layout that was crammed with accessories. Then, during the great train-price inflation of the 1980s, he sold everything and now is retired, living in the sun in Florida.

COLLECTOR SPECIALTIES

Collectors' interests tend to change. As a result, collections grow in odd and unpredictable ways, reflecting shifts in owner focus and level of intensity. Few are static. Fewer still are ever "completed." If collections are subject to continuing modification, then so are collector specialties. Attempting to pin them down can be difficult and risky, but let's try. The following are some representative and fairly common areas in which collectors have specialized during the past several years.

Not many true generalists exist today, even among the old guard. Although some newcomers enter the hobby as generalists, with no specific collecting goals in mind, they soon become inundated by the sheer number of choices. Just too much attractive and well-made new merchandise is on the market, and the supply of older collector pieces is plentiful. Assuming unlimited resources and adequate storage space, attempting to buy and catalog all of it would amount to a full-time job.

Those hobbyists who do maintain the broad generalist perspective have to be selective. They limit their collections to those trains they find most appealing in each of the various groups or categories. This in itself is a kind of specialization and a very individual one.

Collectors must narrow their focus to a manageable field if they wish to enjoy depth. Several logical and acceptable ways of reducing the scope of a collection exist; they lead enthusiasts to specific concentrations:

• One particular gauge or scale
• A specific manufacturer's products
• A certain era of toy train production
• One class of rolling stock or an individual road name

Chuck Brasher is a Standard gauge specialist who likes to operate his equipment. The trains and accessories that aren't set up or ready to roll on his 20 x 40-foot attic layout are proudly displayed on shelves behind it.

Many collectors choose to specialize in these ways. However, a collection can still become cumbersome even when defined by one or more of these areas of concentration. For example, one of the most popular categories today is Lionel postwar O gauge. It combines the first three items in the list above and includes trains that were manufactured between 1945 and 1969, the year that the Lionel Corporation leased the rights to produce its toy trains to General Mills.

A complete collection of Lionel postwar O gauge would include almost a thousand different items: 211 locomotives and powered units, 403 cars, and 326 accessories. That is just one of each, without variations. Many models had multiple (and collectible) variations, particularly if they were produced over a long period. Then there are the factory prototypes and salesman's samples so dear to the hearts of collectors. A truly definitive collection of postwar Lionel trains might well entail between two and three thousand pieces.

Few hobbyists can afford to collect all the postwar O gauge Lionel, even without the variations, so they concentrate on certain types of trains within the broader category. This is the point at which collections begin to take on unique or highly individualized characteristics. Some people will zero in on locomotives or boxcars or operating accessories; others will collect complete original sets. Those with a flair for the unusual may be attracted to oddities, rare variations, samples, and factory errors. The range of possibilities is almost limitless.

At the other extreme, some collectors seem to be more comfortable specializing in a fairly small and well-defined universe, such as Lionel OO gauge. Produced from 1938 to 1942, this line featured only one basic locomotive and four freight cars, although

Ward Kimball, a longtime animation artist for Disney Studios, has been collecting toy trains since the 1940s. His collection contains many rare American and European pieces from the late 19th and early 20th centuries. Shown here are some of the European trains and accessories on display and in operation in part of his train building.

Even the tin lithographed trains by Marx, Hafner, American Flyer, and Unique have become respectable collector's items, as shown by this view of a part of Don Simonini's extensive collection.

each had several variations. A complete collection includes only 27 pieces.

Road name and rolling stock class collections are also popular. Some people like to collect models displaying the markings and heralds of a favorite real railroad, such as the Santa Fe or the Union Pacific. In recent years, fans have become particularly interested in collecting examples of those roads that have been swallowed up by corporate mergers—New York Central, Great Northern, and Baltimore & Ohio, among others. Road name collectors rarely concentrate on a gauge, scale, or manufacturer. Usually their collections present a cross section of all of them.

Collections of different classes of rolling stock are interesting because of their variety in size and origin. Some collectors concentrate on steam locomotives. Others like diesels or crane cars or cabooses. Collections of this kind can be colorful, particularly those that display diesel locomotives or boxcars.

Other collectors I have known specialized in foreign trains, windup trains, lithographed sheet-metal trains, live steamers, circus trains, trackless pull toys, and trains associated with cartoon characters. It wouldn't surprise me if someone on a tight budget was collecting transformer handles or track pins. It's all fair game. The objects collected are determined by the individual's taste, space, and pocketbook. Nothing else accounts for the many and diverse specialties pursued by toy train collectors. If it runs on rails, and the manufacturer made more than one copy, somebody will eventually start collecting it.

An old Lionel dealer display makes a great showcase for treasured trains, even if it takes up a lot of space. Ed Dougherty uses this one from 1949.

STORING AND DISPLAYING YOUR TRAINS

WHAT ARE you going to do with all those trains? As your collection grows, this question becomes more and more pressing. How you choose to deal with it may well be one of the most important decisions of your collecting career. When you own one or two trains, the mantelpiece, bookcase, or dining room plate rail may work just fine. However, collections usually outgrow these spaces soon. Then storage and display can become a serious family problem.

Suggestions from others, even positive and well-intentioned ones, may not prove practical. While there are probably as many solutions as there are train collectors, the major consideration in keeping peace on the premises is that you do something before your prized possessions become household nuisances. By then, no amount of sweet salve and diplomacy will work.

One major cause of inertia among new collectors is confusion about the optimum conditions for storing trains. Many would have you believe that toy trains should be kept only in a temperature- and humidity-controlled environment, free of dust and pollution, and away from direct sunlight. The "ideal" storage facility that they envision would look something like the "clean room" down at the computer factory.

Other collectors seriously debate the harmful effects of artificial lighting on painted and lithographed finishes. The raging argument over incandescent versus fluorescent fixtures for the train room leads ultimately to the conclusion that vintage toy trains may best be displayed in the dark!

I wouldn't even be surprised to hear some horticulturist recommend talking to your trains, or a retired dentist, disc jockey, or elevator operator insist that they should be serenaded with soothing music at least once a week. Such is the nature of the mythology and the magnitude of the misinformation.

Be realistic and practical. Separate the facts from the folklore. These trains were produced as toys. Although not indestructible, they are inherently tough. Many of the storage legends spring from the simple observation that trains kept in dry attics for long periods generally survived better than those stored in damp basements.

High humidity can cause rust, but it is easily controllable. Unless the water trickles down your basement walls and forms puddles on the floor all summer, chances are that a couple of small dehumidifiers are sufficient to provide a healthy storage environment. Ask your helpful hardware man about the correct capacity for your basement.

Temperature, too, is only a factor in the extreme. In torrid climates, where attics get hot enough to make a camel faint, damage to plastic and rubber parts can occur. On the other hand, trains are rarely subject to frostbite, and I have never heard of one freezing to death in North America!

As far as dust, pollution, and direct sunlight are concerned, look for practical solutions. Household dust can easily be brushed or wiped off if it hasn't been allowed to accumulate for years. The residue of air pollution, even tobacco smoke, can be cleaned from exposed surfaces with soap and water or furniture polish. To minimize the fading effects of direct sunlight, either pull down your shades or store your stuff in a different room.

In other words, don't be too concerned about what you may have heard regarding the proper care and feeding of toy trains. Just enjoy your collection. Life is short.

DISPLAYING YOUR TRAINS

In the best of all worlds, every train in your collection would be on display at all times. Sometimes, though,

Three rails are integral parts of the aluminum extrusion that forms Rail Rax shelving. The 6-foot sections can be attached with screws to the wall studs. The anodized finish never needs paint.

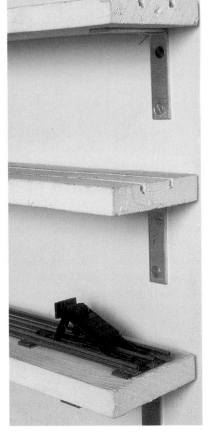

Steel angle brackets and common 1 x 4 boards held in place with flathead wood screws make simple, inexpensive display shelves. To keep models secure, cut flangeway grooves lengthwise into the lumber or mount old track sections on it.

1 GA. CW. 1912-14

C. 1913

MARKLIN

N 1 GA. ELEC. 1913

Commercial shelf brackets and standards are popular with toy train collectors because they are sturdy and the shelves can be moved up or down if necessary.

that doesn't work out. There just isn't enough shelf space for everything in the average American home, no matter how carefully that space is used. Because of this, most collectors have learned to be selective in what they have available for viewing.

Often collectors choose to display only their favorite items and leave the rest boxed and stored. Some have a rotating display system, changing the items on the shelves periodically, according to the season, preferences of expected guests, or whatever. (This idea has beneficial side effects because of the natural tendency to dust things before packing them away.)

Collectors display their trains using many different physical means. Some are dictated by cost; others are limited by the manual skills of the individual. Let's examine some of the more popular ones.

Glass cases. These are undoubtedly the ultimate display method. Here trains are treated with the dignity of artifacts in a museum. The glass protects them from dust and the prying fingers of visitors. The cases

can be lighted in sophisticated ways, thereby enhancing the jewel-like qualities of each piece. Of course, few hobbyists can afford the expense and the space to house an entire collection in this way, so some use the glass cases in combination with conventional wall shelving. Only the most interesting or special items are placed under glass.

Rail Rax. This is the brand name of a line of extruded aluminum shelves specifically designed to display trains. Sold in 6-foot sections, the shelves accommodate all popular track gauges. Because of the unique construction of these shelves, supporting brackets are not necessary. The Rail Rax units can be drilled and screwed directly into wall studs. Their shiny anodized finish eliminates the need for painting. An excellent though expensive product.

Metal shelf brackets and standards. These are available in most hardware or building supply stores. Because they are easy to install and reasonably priced, such rigs are widely used for train displays. The

This collector stores his boxed Lionel and American Flyer sets next to the fireplace in his living room. It works for him. John Wickland collection.

brackets and standards ("stringers," if you will) come in four or five metallic finishes and accommodate shelves of different widths. The distances between shelves can be adjusted to meet the changing requirements of a growing collection.

Some collectors use the prefinished shelves sold with the brackets and standards, while others prefer to make their own out of plywood, particle board, or even common lumber. The choice of shelving material is usually dictated by the pocketbook. Four-inch-wide shelves are popular with O and S gauge collectors. Standard gauge and G scale displays require widths of 6 or 8 inches.

Angle brackets and boards. Some of the best O gauge collections I've seen stood on common 1 x 4s, supported by flat steel 90-degree-angle brackets. Shelves constructed in this way are sturdy, and they can be made attractive in spite of their simplicity. You can paint them to match the wall, so they blend in. Furthermore, these shelves can be spaced closer together than the prefabricated bracket-and-standard type because the supporting members are flat and won't get in the way of items on the shelf below.

The themes illustrated above have many variations, and you will undoubtedly come up with one of your own to work your collection into the space you have. Here is one strong suggestion, however, that applies to all train displays. It was made years ago by Joshua Lionel Cowen himself. He insisted that all of his trains be displayed standing on track. This went for his own showrooms and all the train departments in stores across the country. It was his firm conviction that trains looked silly standing on their flanges and the only way to convey action and to maintain straight-line symmetry was by putting track under them. J. L. was right!

This is undoubtedly the reason that Rail Rax extrusions have simulated rails built right in. It's also why many collectors attach surplus track sections to their shelves. That method makes good use of all those old, rusty tracks that seem to accumulate everywhere. Spray them with cheap aluminum paint and fasten them to your shelving. They will make your trains look even better.

If you don't want track on your shelves, you can achieve the same effect by cutting parallel grooves lengthwise in the shelf boards. These should be properly gauged and made deep enough to accept the full wheel flanges. Some collectors prefer this method because it saves vertical space.

CLEANING, RESTORING, AND RECYCLING YOUR TRAINS

ALTHOUGH IT'S NOT for everyone, restoring old trains can be one of most rewarding facets of the hobby. Whether you decide to restore, what you choose to restore, and to what degree depend on you. If you have the inclination, this chapter provides techniques for putting the shine back into those old trains.

REFURBISHING ROLLING STOCK

To clean or not to clean? There are two divergent schools of thought on this. To some purist collectors, just blowing dust off an old toy train is an act of desecration. They want to have all the original dirt on every item. They think the grime, caked-on grease, fingerprints, rug fuzz, and cat hair show the history of the piece and should not be disturbed. Needless to say, they feel the same way about repairs. If the train happens to be missing some parts when they acquire it—a coupler, ladder, side rod, wheel, the roof—they just prop it up as best they can and proudly display it "as found."

At the other end are those collectors who tinker, doctor, and touch up everything they find that isn't in excellent condition. They maintain that toy trains were bright and colorful when new, so they try to return all of theirs to a condition resembling factory freshness. If that requires cleaning, fixing, replacing parts, or even repainting, fine. Often they get carried away trying to improve upon everything they own, whether it needs it or not.

I have a hard time with both extremes. I find no pleasure in viewing train rooms filled with what appear to be rows of fatigued and wounded battle wagons returning from war, decked out in dust gray and crud brown. On the other hand, I'm not turned on by shelves that resemble some gaudy, old-fashioned department store train display the week before Christmas, particularly if the paint jobs convey the impression that Santa's elves had been distilling the reindeer feed.

There has to be some middle ground—a sane compromise that borrows the best elements from both extremes. It is hard to formulate rules or guidelines about when cleaning or restoring a train is appropriate. That determination is a matter of individual preference.

I suppose because I grew up in an American household that prescribed daily baths, laundered clothing, and scrubbed floors, I like to clean every piece before I put it into my collection. While I don't usually touch up nicks and scratches with paint, if a train is marginal or unsightly, I will restore it.

Some people clean and restore trains professionally. They have their own methods, skills, trade secrets, and special equipment to accomplish the job. Although only a layman at this, I have managed through years of trial and error to develop my own techniques, which I'll pass along. They involve only common household tools and products that are easy to use. And, to borrow a quotation from well-known sports figure Tommy Lasorda, "If I can do it, you can do it!"

The basic equipment and supplies helpful in cleaning old toy trains can be obtained inexpensively at hardware and building supply stores.

CLEANING

Usually, a little cleaning is all that's needed to greatly improve the appearance of your toy trains. I've found the following tools and products helpful in cleaning trains of all kinds. You may wish to augment and enhance the operation with your own pet methods or equipment. Just remember to proceed from the mild to the more harsh or severe and to use the cleaning products sparingly. Everything listed below has been used many times with good results. Be careful anyway.

Unless the train is merely dusty or superficially dirty, partial disassembly is recommended. This is particularly important for locomotives and operating cars or accessories, which include electrical or mechanical parts water may damage. Generally, painted surfaces are cleaned with different products than unpainted ones.

Tools and equipment
• Sink with warm running water. It should have some kind of stopper for soaking. Laundry tubs are ideal for larger projects.
• Paper towels
• Rags. Have a variety of textures on hand, ranging from old T-shirts to terrycloth hand towels.
• Cotton swabs
• Pipe cleaners
• Toothbrushes. Old, high-mileage ones that have become soft and pliable are best. I like to have at least two, one for use with detergents and waxes and the other for greasy or oily jobs.
• Steel wool. Get several balls ranging from fine to medium coarseness. These are effective on lightly rusted surfaces.
• Sandpaper. Fine to medium grit, both wet and dry. Use this instead of steel wool in some applications.
• Wire brush. This is for attacking heavier rust. A wire wheel is great if you have one.
• Hair dryer. Useful, but not essential. Excellent for drying parts quickly after washing and rinsing. It can also be used to heat surfaces slightly, which is helpful when removing mildew or old wax.

Supplies
• Mild bar soap. Use Ivory or a similar brand on delicate or fragile painted surfaces, such as old enamel already starting to check or crack. Soap hands and gently rub the surface with your fingertips. Rinse well with warm water.
• Dish detergent. Any brand will work for general cleaning. You don't need the high-priced stuff with all the additives. Fill sink with a mild solution in warm water. Soak pieces for a minute or two, then wash as you would individual dishes, with a cloth or your fingers. Use cotton swabs and pipe cleaners for hard-to-reach places. A toothbrush may be used on heavy accu-

Many toy trains can be cleaned with a solution of dish detergent and warm water. After disassembling the model, soak the body parts for a minute or two. If necessary, attack heavy dirt on enameled surfaces with an old toothbrush. Finish by rinsing it well.

mulations, but don't brush vigorously. Rinse well with warm water.
• Toothpaste. A simple gel is good; you don't need fluorides and germ fighters. Use this only as a last resort on ground-in dirt that dish detergent won't budge. Work into a lather. Brush lightly. Stay away from all lettering. Rinse well in warm water.
• Wax furniture polish. Pledge or a similar brand can be used by itself on light dirt and dust. It works well as a finishing coat on shiny painted surfaces that have been washed in detergent. Apply as directed. Buff to a sheen with a clean cloth.
• Nonwax furniture polish. Duster-Plus or a similar brand can also be used by itself on light dirt and dust, and as a finishing coat for dull or matte painted surfaces washed in detergent. Apply as directed. Wipe with a clean cloth.
• Automotive combination cleaner-wax. Kit is about the best on the market for our purposes. It is effective on badly oxidized enamel surfaces. Use by itself as directed or as a finishing coat after washing in detergent. A clean cloth is essential.
• Automotive chrome cleaner-polish. Any brand will do to shine nickel, brass, and copper trim pieces and to remove rust from chemically blackened surfaces. Be

sure all the residue is removed with furniture polish or penetrating oil.

• Degreasing solvent. Mineral spirits is the best; buy it by the gallon because you will find dozens of uses for it. This is useful for soaking unpainted greasy and dirty parts, such as wheels, trucks, couplers, chemically blackened castings, and sheet-metal parts. Simply brush and soak them until they come clean. Mineral spirits can be used straight on locomotive motors and accessory mechanisms. Brush it on or dip (do not soak!) the whole thing and let it drip-dry. Use a toothbrush to loosen the dirt and cotton swabs to mop up. Keep brushing or dipping until the runoff is no longer black and dirty. (Caution: Mineral spirits is a combustible liquid. Use in a ventilated area, away from sparks or flames. Be sure locomotive mechanisms are thoroughly dry before trying to run them.)

• Penetrating oil spray. Use WD-40 or CRC 556 by itself to clean lightly dirty parts and as a finishing coat after soaking a part in mineral spirits. Both products are mild rust-removers that leave a light lubricant as residual protection. They should not be used to replace regular oil or grease on bearings and axles, however.

I've used all of these products and techniques for years; however, because there are many different types of painted surfaces and because some paint may have "softened" with age, I suggest that you test each piece before going ahead. Try the cleaning technique on an inconspicuous place first, such as the inside.

Treat all lettered surfaces as fragile, whether they have been heat-stamped, rubber-stamped, or decaled. Never brush or rub hard. Decals should not be soaked in anything, even water. They can loosen and come off. Use cotton swabs to clean lettered areas.

Mildew is particularly hard to remove. On surfaces not easily damaged, try a household cleaner, such as Formula 409, and a soft brush. Flush well with water after cleaning. On more delicate surfaces, try using a hair dryer. Heating the surface will sometimes loosen the mildew so it can be brushed or swabbed away. This doesn't always work. Be patient and experiment. Don't be disappointed if some of the mildew doesn't come off. You may just have to live with it.

Harsh rust removers, such as Naval Jelly, are categorically not recommended unless you plan to refinish the train. They do remove rust, but they also attack paint, plating, and chemical coloring agents. If you intend to repaint, read on.

ROLLING STOCK RECLAMATION

Extreme cases require drastic measures. If your train looks even halfway presentable after cleaning, leave it that way for a while. Try getting used to it. If, after staring at it for months, the train remains an eyesore to you, by all means do something about it. However, once a restoration project is undertaken, there is no turning back.

Always rinse an item well and blot it dry with a clean paper towel. Then you are ready to reassemble the car.

Reclaiming old metal trains is not as difficult as many people imagine. As with the cleaning techniques discussed above, you don't need expensive equipment. Simple household tools and products work well. Anyone can master the skills involved with patience and practice. You just have to overcome the inertia and the fear of failure. If you botch the job, just do it over until you get it right. No one needs to know the difference. What's important is to get started and to keep at it, learning and developing your techniques with each successful project.

Types of renovation

Restoration. This involves returning a train to a condition closely approximating the way it was when it left the factory. All lines and surfaces should be smooth. Correct paint colors, lettering, and trim parts are essential. A good restoration is a faithful re-creation of original condition down to the last detail.

Representation. This includes the same integrity of detail but involves making the piece represent something different from what it was originally. This is most often accomplished by changing the color, lettering, or trim parts to make the representation simulate another piece of the same basic configuration. Strict fidelity to the piece being represented is important.

Recycled piece. This refers mainly to turning an unsightly "junker" into something usable and appealing with no particular concern for the original or even a prototype. This is by far the most common kind of renovation.

The examples in the photos show all three of these. The Lionel O gauge 259E locomotive and four-wheel passenger cars are basic restorations, returned to a condition approximating the originals when new. The black 2855 tank car is a representation made from a more common 2555 original. The Santa Fe Hudson was recycled from a stock Lionel 2055 in less-than-perfect shape.

BASIC TECHNIQUES

Take the train apart completely. There is no shortcut around total disassembly if you want the

This battered Lionel O gauge 259E locomotive was an excellent candidate for full restoration. The author discovered it in a junk box at a local train meet.

finished product to look right. Get down to fundamental components. If you think you'll have trouble remembering how everything fits together, make notes or drawings so you can retrace your steps later. Major bending and straightening can be undertaken at this point, with final smoothing and touching up done after the parts have been stripped.

Find a matching paint color. Clean a section of the original painted surface and compare it with paint chips for commercial spray-can enamels. The various brands are all slightly different. Shop around. Some of the standard colors come amazingly close.

If you can't find a satisfactory match, try automotive paint stores. They have hundreds of color chips in their catalogs and often can supply the correct shade. As a last resort, you can have your color custom-mixed. This is expensive, and you will need some sort of sprayer to apply it.

Allegedly authentic toy train colors are available from several mail-order suppliers. Although I haven't tried them all, the ones that I have used were disappointing. Therefore, find your own match if possible.

Strip the individual pieces. Once you have the matching paint, you can get down to bare metal. Dozens of products will strip off old paint, but some work better than others. You can safely use any household semipaste paint remover, but use caution, wear gloves and protective clothing, and avoid spilling any remover on surfaces you don't want stripped. Remove all traces of the old paint, even if more than one application is needed. Then wash away every bit of the stripper.

Most commercial strippers will attack and ruin plastic. I remove paint from plastic pieces by soaking them in a strong solution of laundry detergent and water. After some time the paint will loosen and come off. Occasional scrubbing with a coarse brush hastens the process.

Do all finishing touches before painting. Any metal surfaces should be made as smooth as possible before applying paint. Use whatever tools you have available to perform this basic "body and fender" work. Ease the metal back into shape. Keep your tools as "soft" as practical. Use wood blocks to cushion hammer blows. Line your vise jaws and pliers with cardboard. Dents that stretch the metal too far may have to be filled in.

Commercial epoxy fillers or good old automotive body putty can be used to plug holes and fill dents. Automotive "glazing and spot putty" can be used by

Quality restoration requires that you completely disassemble a model, as the author did with the Lionel 259E locomotive and tender. All the parts of the 259E locomotive and its tender have been stripped, straightened, and filled. Now they're ready to be painted.

Completely restored and repainted, the 259E locomotive and 1588T
tender look as nice as they did the day they left the Lionel factory.

itself on minor rough spots or as a finishing surface over body putty. When everything has dried, sand it smooth with fine-grit paper.

Apply the paint. Whether you choose to prime is up to you. Priming makes the finish coat adhere better. Some primers can be sanded and allow for correction of fine blemishes. The lighter colors tend to be transparent and require multiple coats anyway. Chances are the train wasn't primed originally, so if you are a purist, it is your call. If possible, prime with the same brand of paint as your finish coat to avoid incompatibility between the two layers.

Practice to get the hang of spray-painting. Work slowly. It isn't difficult, but it requires trial-and-error experimentation on expendable metal objects or surfaces first. Be sure you have adequate ventilation because the fumes can pose a health hazard if inhaled directly.

Follow the directions on the spray can carefully. Be certain that the paint is well mixed by shaking the can vigorously for at least the duration recommended by the manufacturer. You can't overmix the paint in an aerosol can, but you can undermix it. That can cause matching problems.

Most spray enamels will be dry to the touch in half an hour and set up in a day, but it may take weeks for the paint to really harden. Baking accelerates the hardening, but it can be dangerous if tried in a home oven. Most stove controls are not accurate at the low recommended temperature of about 150 degrees. If the oven gets too hot, the paint will blister, sag, or ignite. If you are in a hurry, a better alternative is to place your freshly painted pieces in direct sunlight indoors for a couple of hours.

Lettering. Most original lettering was applied by rubber stamp or decal. Reproduction decals and dry-transfer lettering sets to replace the rubber stampings are available for some of the more popular models. Check with your local hobby shop or order direct from one of the suppliers listed in the appendix. If the let-

tering for your particular train is not available, you may have to improvise.

Reassembly. This step shouldn't be tried until the paint has fully hardened. Work carefully, touching the painted surfaces as little as possible. Working on a folded towel instead of a hard surface helps to avoid accidental scuffs and nicks. Wipe off fingerprints with a damp cloth.

RESTORING THE 259E LOCOMOTIVE AND 1588T TENDER

Fortunately, all the trim parts were still on the locomotive, although the front and rear trucks were missing. That posed no problem, since reproductions were readily available. The "Lionel Lines" plates on the side of the tender were badly scratched, so I decided to replace them as well. Everything else used in this restoration was original.

First, I took the locomotive apart completely. Then I dunked the mechanism (motor, drive wheels, reverse unit, and so on) and in a mineral spirits bath and brushed it until it came clean. The insulation had hardened and broken off two exposed wires, so I replaced them. Next, I lightly sprayed the wheels and side frames with WD-40 and tested the mechanism. It worked, but the reverse unit was erratic. A few squirts of TV tuner cleaner (available from Radio Shack) directly on the drum cured that problem. The axles and bearings were lubricated, and the mechanism was tested again. This time it ran like new, so I put it aside.

For the next step, I straightened the sheet metal. Much of this work was done by hand. Any dents and bends that wouldn't respond to persuasion from my fingers and thumbs had to be dealt with more severely. Using a pair of needlenose pliers, a small ball peen hammer, a flat bar anvil, two hardwood blocks, and a dowel the size of the boiler front, I eliminated the rest of the kinks.

Next, I removed the trim parts and painted all surfaces stripped with a heavy-bodied paint remover

The 2055 locomotive and tender before undergoing their makeover.

(check your local paint or hardware store). Two applications were needed to remove all traces.

I dressed heavily rusted areas with a wire wheel mounted in an electric drill. Then I rubbed all the surfaces with fine steel wool. A few wrinkles and pits that remained in the tender sides were filled with glazing and spot putty and sanded until smooth. Then I used a fresh tack cloth (gauze-like material permeated with a sticky substance that's available at any paint store) to remove all residue and dust from the surfaces to be painted.

The ornamental bell (riveted to the boiler), the drawbar pin (riveted to the frame), and the crosshead guides (riveted to the steamchests) were carefully masked with tape. These nickel-plated parts are not easily removed, so I decided to leave them attached during painting. Meanwhile, I cleaned all detachable trim parts with automotive chrome polish, buffed them to a shine, and sprayed them with WD-40.

I applied a coat of Krylon Charcoal Black Primer to all surfaces, inside and out. Because this primer can

be sanded, minor blemishes missed before may be smoothed away. I was lucky this time: There weren't any. I let the primer dry for 24 hours.

The next day, I inspected the primed surfaces, which I then dusted with the tack cloth and pronounced ready for the finish coats. I chose Krylon Glossy Black Enamel because the color and sheen of the paint closely approximate those of the original. Several light, dusting coats work better than one heavy one on curved surfaces such as locomotive boilers, so everything was given three coats of paint, with one hour of drying between. The pieces were inspected for uniformity of luster and set aside for a week.

Reassembly was done carefully on top of a folded cloth towel to protect the new paint from accidental scuffs. Although the paint had dried, it still hadn't hardened thoroughly in so short a time.

RECYCLING A 2055 STEAM LOCOMOTIVE

This venerable old horse, too battered and bruised to be a collector's prize yet still energetic and serviceable

Here are the disassembled parts of the 2055 locomotive and tender before painting.

The locomotive and tender, recycled into a Santa Fe Hudson, are now ready for hi-rail service.

underneath, was recycled into a "hi-rail runner," a reasonable replica of the Santa Fe Hudson. The conversion was a natural because the Lionel model was loosely patterned after this prototype.

First, I cleaned, tuned, and lubricated the locomotive mechanism and the whistle. The burned-out coil heater in the smoke generator was replaced with a conversion unit, changing it from a pill-burner to the more modern liquid smoke. (See the next chapter for step-by-step details.)

Next, I stripped the plastic tender shell by soaking it for three days in a strong solution of Ajax laundry detergent and water. The main locomotive castings were dealt with in the usual way—repeated applications of heavy-bodied paint remover—until all traces of the original paint had been flushed away. That Lionel locomotive enamel from the 1950s was really tough; apparently they intended it to stay on forever!

One marker light and both pilot steps were badly bent, so straightening them came next. Trying to bend old die-cast metal is always a gamble: Will it yield to gentle pressure, or will it break? There is no sure way to determine how the metal has aged until it's too late. Heating is supposed to minimize the risk of breaking, but too much heat will melt the casting. In this case, because the details to be straightened were small, I

used an ordinary disposable cigarette lighter to heat them. A few taps from a small hammer in between heatings returned the castings to their original shape without incident. Perhaps I was lucky?

Instead of priming the locomotive, I gave it two fairly rich coats of Ace Hardware Wrought Iron Flat Black Enamel, about an hour apart. Metal die castings are somewhat porous, so they don't have to be primed first.

The plastic tender shell required a different type of paint, one that wouldn't cause the surface to warp or craze. Testor's Flat Black Enamel was found to be safe, but it didn't match the sheen of the locomotive paint. I corrected this by applying a finish coat of Ace Hardware Polyurethane Satin varnish over it. Since decal lettering had been used on the tender, the recommended practice to dull the shine and blend the surfaces is to apply just such a finish coat anyway.

I completed this recycling by applying the locomotive and tender lettering. I used Woodland Scenics dry transfers on the engine and Walthers decals on the tender to create something new and different for my roster.

MAKING A BLACK 2855 TANK CAR REPRESENTATION

I used a common 2555 tanker as the raw material for this representation of the desirable black 2855. Some

This representation of the desirable 2855 black tank car was made by repainting and lettering a common 2555 car.

58

collectors use facsimiles like this one to fill gaps in their collections until they find an original. Others frown upon the practice. Without getting into the pros and cons of the question, I'll explain how the project was accomplished.

Since the 2555 and 2855 are identical except for paint and lettering, the transformation was simple. After taking the car apart, I stripped the parts and prepared them in the usual way. I cleaned the trucks and trim parts with WD-40.

Then I painted the frame, tank, and dome with Ace Hardware Wrought Iron Flat Black Enamel. After those parts had dried, I applied Kraemer Reproduction Decals in the appropriate places, using a photograph of the 2855 car as a guide.

To dull the decal shine and blend the surfaces, I sprayed the tank and dome with Ace Hardware Polyurethane Satin Varnish. I let everything dry thoroughly before starting the reassembly.

(Sometimes inexperienced buyers are unable to distinguish skillful representations from originals. This is why the TCA and other collecting organizations require that restorations and representations sold at their meets be clearly identified as such. Attempting to pass one off as an original is unethical. Under certain circumstances it can also be illegal.)

RESTORING THE 629 AND 630 FOUR-WHEEL PASSENGER CARS

Having completed the restoration of the 259E locomotive and 1588T tender, I needed a set of appropriate cars to make a train. Three pallid Pullmans and an observation car were soon spotted and rescued from a dusty box at a swap meet. Although not as battered as the locomotive had been, the cars sported major paint chips and rust. Their red color had faded several shades, perhaps from the sun. While these cars were on the border between cleanable and restorable condition, I decided on a full restoration to match the engine.

I relied on the same techniques and products. The sheet metal was stripped and then straightened by hand and with the ball peen hammer and anvil. The trim parts and wheels were cleaned and de-rusted with chrome polish and the wire wheel.

The roofs and bodies were primed with two coats of Krylon Ruddy Brown Primer and finished with Krylon Cherry Red Enamel. While the cars were too sun-faded to make a visual match, I knew from previous experience that this Krylon color closely approximates the shade of red that Lionel used in the early 1930s when the cars were made.

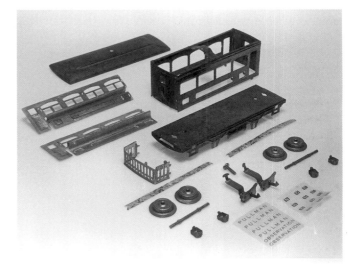

Here is one of the passenger cars, disassembled and ready to be painted.

Next, I primed the window and door inserts with Ace Hardware Neutral Gray Primer and finished them with three coats of Krylon Pastel Yellow Enamel. (Light colors don't cover as well as darker ones.) The frames took one heavy coat of Ace Hardware Wrought Iron Flat Black Enamel. When this paint is applied

Gorgeous again, these O gauge passenger cars are ready for many years of operation or display.

liberally in one thick coat, it dries to a semiflat or satin sheen close to the old Lionel look.

The blue mottled celluloid window strips had shrunk with age and broken away from their mooring tabs. I reattached them with Goo, a contact cement that doesn't damage this material. After the paint had aged for about a week, I applied Bennett Dry Transfer Lettering. Then I reassembled the cars.

Servicing, Lubricating, and Tuning Up Lionel Locomotives

WHILE THE EXAMPLE used in this chapter is one of the most common of the spur-geared Lionel locomotive mechanisms, the suggestions, techniques, and theories can be more universally applied to almost any engine designed for AC operation. In most cases, cleaning, lubricating, and some tuning up will bring an old toy train back to life, regardless of its age. Physical damage caused by misuse, mishandling, or deterioration is another matter. In those instances, a competent service technician should be consulted. However, first-echelon maintenance can be performed on a basically sound unit by anyone with patience and a few household tools.

This circuit diagram was originally published by Lionel for use by its network of Authorized Service Stations. It shows how locomotives with three-position sequence reverse mechanisms, headlights, and smoke generators are wired. The circuit for the typical whistle tender is also shown. Study it before you begin your project, and refer to it as you go along. If the wiring of your train varies from that shown in the diagram, make a note.

Step One: Disassembly
Separate the locomotive boiler and steam chest castings from the basic operating mechanism (motor, drive wheels, and smoke generator assembly). Although each locomotive is slightly different, these parts are usually held together with machine screws or bolts and nuts. The drive rods will also have to come off. Make notes or drawings as you go along so you can retrace your steps during reassembly. Work slowly and carefully, trying not to force anything.

Step Two: Cleaning
Use a degreasing solvent such as mineral spirits to wash the entire mechanism. Apply it liberally with a paintbrush, working loose old dirt and grease deposits.

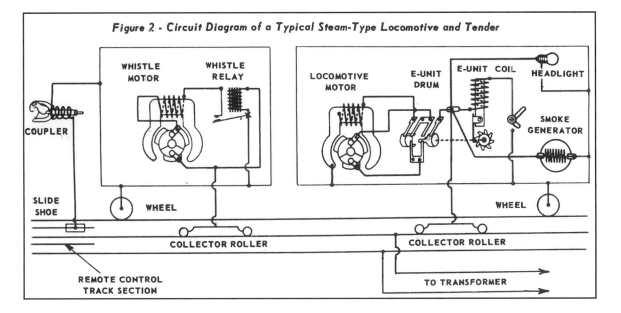

Figure 2 - Circuit Diagram of a Typical Steam-Type Locomotive and Tender

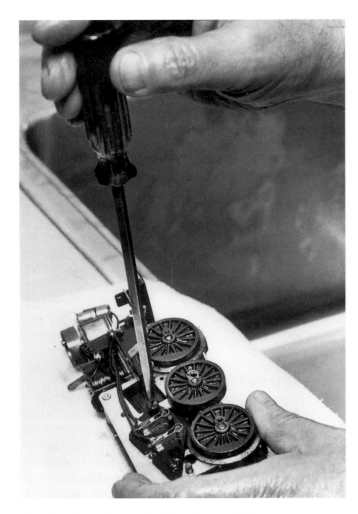

Most brush plates are held in place with two screws.

Remove all the dirt and grease from the mechanism, both inside and out, using a paintbrush dipped in mineral spirits. Repeat this procedure until the mechanism appears clean and the solvent runoff is clear.

After removing the brush plate and brushes, clean out the brush wells with a cotton swab soaked with solvent.

You may dip the unit if you wish, but don't soak it in the solvent. Repeat the operation until the solvent runoff is clear. Allow the mechanism to air-dry thoroughly for at least a few hours. Make sure there are no traces of residual dirt, dust, or fuzz. Mop up with cotton swabs, if necessary.

STEP THREE: COMMUTATOR AND BRUSHES

Remove the brush plate, which usually is held in place by two screws, being careful not to lose the brushes and springs. The brushes are the two cylindrical pieces of carbon that fit into wells or sleeves on the brush plate. In operation, they are held against the rotating armature commutator face by spring tension. On some brush plates, the springs are firmly attached to the sleeves that hold the brushes. On others, fine coil springs within the brush wells exert pressure.

Worn brushes and bad springs are among the most frequent causes of poor motor performance. Replace them if new brushes and springs are available. If they aren't, you may have to adjust the old ones to provide as much efficiency as possible. The springs should exert pressure, thrusting the brushes firmly against the commutator face. The brushes should be about the same length, with the ends flat and square (90-degree angle) with the sides. Coil springs may be adjusted by gently stretching them. Brush ends may be flattened by rubbing them on sandpaper or a fine file.

The brushes must move freely within their holders. Clean the brush wells or sleeves by spraying their

The reverse unit is that coil of wire with a lever attached to it. Remove it with care.

Top: Spray the commutator face with TV tuner cleaner and mop up with cotton swabs. Bottom: Repeat this procedure until the swabs stop picking up dirt.

Reinstall the brush plate with care. Sometimes, because of the spring tension on the brushes, it is easier to hold the brush plate in a horizontal position, as shown here, and then bring the mechanism down on top of it.

insides with TV tuner cleaner (available from Radio Shack) and following with a cotton swab. If you plan to reuse the old brushes and springs, spray them with

the same product and wipe with a paper towel. Remove every bit of that black residue. Never lubricate these surfaces.

Next, dress the commutator face. In most cases, a few sprays with TV tuner cleaner, followed by mop-ups with clean cotton swabs, should be all that is necessary. However, if this treatment doesn't eliminate all the circular black streaks, you'll need to rub the surface gently with fine emery paper until the only color visible is bright copper. Then, with a round wood toothpick, clean out the three slots on the commutator face.

Slide the brushes and springs back into their holders. Then reinstall the brush plate assembly.

STEP FOUR: REVERSE UNIT

The reverse unit is another common source of trouble that often can be corrected by careful cleaning. The symptoms are malfunctions in the familiar "forward, neutral, reverse, neutral" sequence.

The reverse unit (also known as an "E-unit") is the coil with a lever on it that sticks out above most Lionel locomotive mechanisms. It is usually held in place by one sheet-metal screw (sometimes two) and is easily removed from its mooring. The unit consists of two sets of finger contacts and a rotating drum that also has a set of contacts on it. The drum has ratchet-like teeth around its middle. A pawl, attached to a solenoid plunger, advances the drum each time track power is interrupted.

The drum and finger contacts accumulate dirt and oxidation in normal use, and this can cripple a locomotive. A few squirts of TV tuner cleaner often take care of it. Spray the cleaner directly on the drum and mop up gently with a cotton swab.

Advance the drum by hand and keep spraying cleaner on it until all contact surfaces are clean and shiny. Be extra careful not to bend the finger contacts. Spraying the drum will simultaneously clean the fingers.

Replace the finger contacts if they are worn, pitted, or burned off. Occasionally the plastic used in the

Spray the reverse unit drum with TV tuner cleaner and mop very carefully with a clean cotton swab.

Advance the drum by hand and repeat the process until all contact surfaces have been cleaned.

drum will shrink with age, causing too much play in the action or occasional jamming. Replacement drums are available.

If the solenoid sticks, a few squirts of TV tuner cleaner up the shaft will usually cure it. Never lubricate these surfaces. Reinstall the reverse unit.

Step Five: Check the External Wiring

Using the circuit diagram as a guide, check the external wiring to ensure that it is routed properly and the solder joints are secure. Make sure there are no cracks or gaps in the insulation that could cause short circuits after reassembly.

Burned-out smoke elements can be replaced with new liquid smoke conversion units. These units, available from Lionel parts dealers, are easily and quickly installed.

Step Six: Smoke Generator

The two most common problems with the old pill-type smoke generators are burned-out heater coils and plugged air passages. Often the entire smoke chamber is clogged with unexpended pill residue, which resembles white granite. Sometimes the stuff even drips down onto the piston, freezing it in the cylinder.

The only way to attack this mess is to hack, chip, and scrape it away. Of course, even if the heater coil was intact before you have started, the chances are good it won't survive the cleaning.

Never try to fix the smoke generator or make it work better. If it does not work, don't worry about why, just replace it with one of the new liquid smoke conversion units, available from Lionel parts dealers. They work better than the pill types ever did.

To install the conversion units, just pry off the sheet-metal cover, rip out the old coil heater and insulation, and chisel away the white residue. Make sure the little air hole isn't clogged and the piston moves in its cylinder. Then plop the new liquid element in place and hook up the wire. That's it.

Step Seven: Lubrication

Many different lubricant products are on the market, some of them formulated specifically for toy trains.

Remove the brush plate and brushes from the whistle motor. Clean the brush wells, brushes, and commutator face as you did the locomotive motor.

Most are good; many are expensive. While it's important that you use something on locomotive axles, bearings, and gears, generic petroleum jelly and all-purpose machine oil work just fine. Whatever you choose, be sure to use it sparingly.

The two most important bearings to lubricate are those at each end of the armature shaft. These are subject to the highest RPM, and have the greatest potential for wear. Lubricate driver axles regularly with one drop dispensed from the end of a wood toothpick. A thin film of grease on the gear teeth is also recommended. Other internal moving parts, such as smoke generator arms, also benefit from occasional light greasing. Toy train engines will last amazingly long if they are just kept lubricated.

Drivers and motor side plates can be made to shine by spraying your toothbrush with WD-40 and scrubbing them.

STEP EIGHT: TESTING AND REASSEMBLY

If you haven't tested the mechanism as you went along during cleaning and tune-up, now is the time to do so. The proof of the pudding is in how the engine performs on the track, not on the workbench.

Give the mechanism a thorough test run to be sure everything is working as it should before you begin reassembly. Then test it again after the locomotive has been put back together. Many people just let the thing run for half an hour or so at this point to be sure no gremlins are lurking in the works.

When you're satisfied with the locomotive's performance, move on to the tender.

STEP NINE: SERVICING THE WHISTLE

After cleaning the whistle case with WD-40 and wiping accumulated dust from the exposed impeller blades with a cotton swab, remove the brush plate and service the whistle motor the same way as you did the locomotive motor.

Spray the two exposed contacts at the bottom of the relay coil and the top of the relay armature with TV tuner cleaner. Then wipe them carefully with an absorbent paper towel.

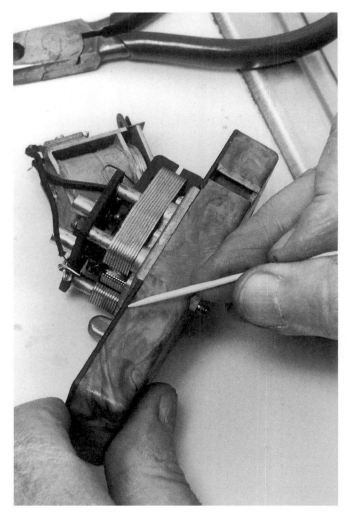

Carefully check for cracks and leaks where the two main pieces of the whistle chamber come together. These can be sealed with household cement or epoxy.

Clean the contacts at the bottom of the whistle relay. If they fail to close properly, bend them slightly.

If possible, lubricate both ends of the whistle motor armature shaft. (On some whistles, only one end of the shaft is accessible.)

Check for loose or broken wires, particularly those leading from the roller pickups. Repair or replace as required.

Test the whistle on the track. If the relay closes when the button is pressed yet the whistle doesn't blow, bend the relay contacts slightly until it works.

If the whistle motor revs up as it should but the sound produced is faint, check for a leak in the whistle chamber. This often happens with age. The gaskets on the older metal chambers dry out. Sometimes a crack in the plastic chambers will develop where the two main pieces were originally glued together. In either case, the leak can be sealed with the application of hard-drying household cement or epoxy. Reassemble the tender and test it again.

That's it. Now you're ready to enjoy your reconditioned, tuned, and well-oiled machine.

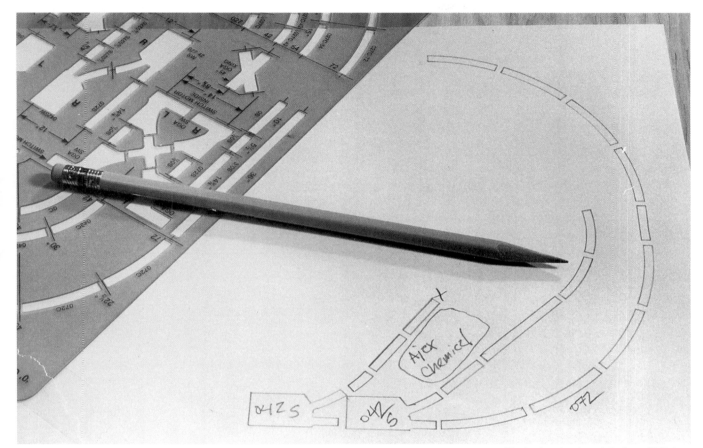

Track planning template from CTT, Inc.

PLANNING YOUR LAYOUT

THE MOST IMPORTANT tool you can use in building your layout is a pencil. Careful, precise planning on paper is essential before you start construction. Although the best-laid track plans may still sometimes turn into bad layouts, bad track plans can never result in good ones.

Before you can seriously plan your dream layout, you must obtain title to the right-of-way, free and clear. This often requires a high degree of domestic diplomacy. (A master's degree in psychology can be helpful too.) Trade-offs and compromises are the key. The bargaining chips that work well depend upon the individual case. Communicate. Talk it over with the whole family before you begin. Be certain that everyone understands the ground rules and the exact space

in question. Make notes. Draw pictures and diagrams if necessary.

Don't try to annex too much or squeeze out more room by doubling up on space. A fiddle yard (a place where you handle cars away from the railroad) hidden in the family room or a lift bridge over the laundry tubs may be an effective way of gaining extra running space in a limited universe, but some might disagree. It upsets their perceived notions of natural order and things in their places.

Be realistic about available space when planning for your favorite railroad activity. Even fairly large layouts do not represent much "real world" real estate, so

Text continues on page 70

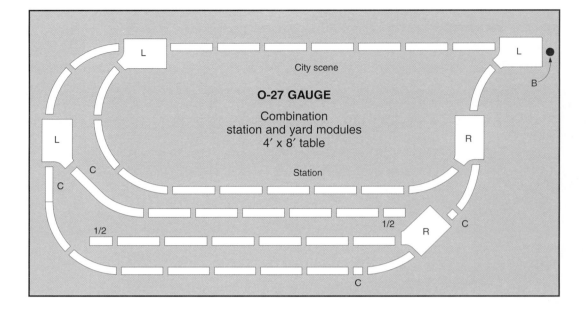

O-27 GAUGE

Combination
station and yard modules
4' x 8' table

City scene

Station

B

L L L R R 1/2 1/2 C C C C

STATION-CENTERED ACTIVITY

This is a complete freight and passenger facility in a small space. It could be one end of a point-to-point system or placed anywhere along the way. Provisions for through trains as well as those stopping or laying over at the station make for great operational possibilities.

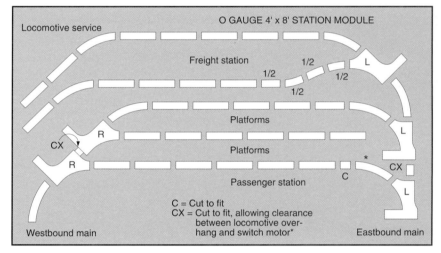

O GAUGE 4' x 8' STATION MODULE

Locomotive service

Freight station

Platforms

Platforms

Passenger station

C = Cut to fit
CX = Cut to fit, allowing clearance between locomotive overhang and switch motor*

Westbound main

Eastbound main

L L L R R CX CX 1/2 1/2 1/2 1/2 C *

YARD AND INDUSTRIAL ACTIVITY

Seven yard and industrial spurs provide a great amount of switching activity. The main line enters on one side of the module and exits on the other, providing diagonal interests to the picture. Six turnouts leading to the main line will prevent the engineer from highballing through the section.

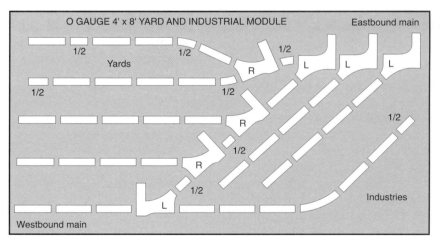

O GAUGE 4' x 8' YARD AND INDUSTRIAL MODULE

Eastbound main

Yards

Industries

Westbound main

R R R L L L L 1/2 1/2 1/2 1/2 1/2 1/2 1/2

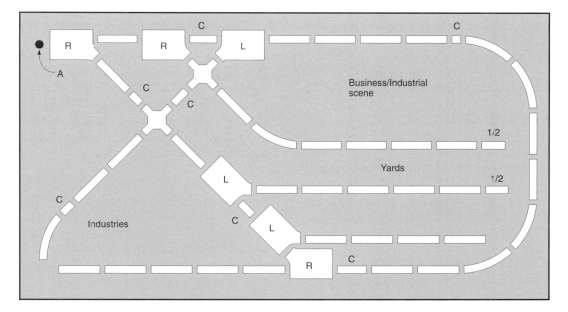

COMBINATION OF ACTIVITIES

Complete point-to-point layout on two 4′ x 8′ modules

The track plans above and at the top of page 68 contain all varieties of activity—stations, yards, industries, connected by a stretch of single-track open road (between points A and B). The size and configuration of the open road section will depend upon available space. A passing siding some-where on the open road would add operational interest. The two modules may be joined together at points A and B if desired, by inserting one section of straight track between the switches. In that case, the industrial sidings can be extended or modified to fit the table space.

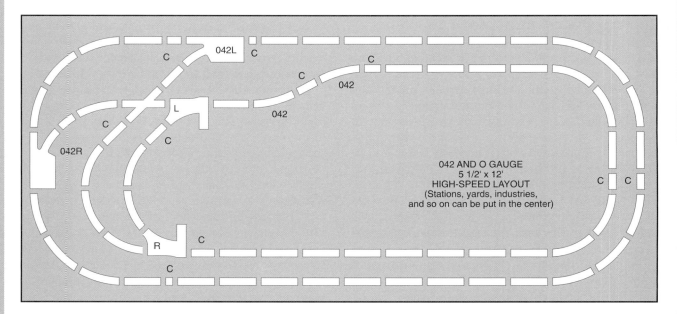

HIGH-SPEED RUNNING

This layout is about as versatile as they come. It can be a long two-lap oval or two individual ovals, depending upon how the switches are thrown. The outer rails are O42 for high-speed running, the inner rails are regular O gauge. Any number of spurs and sidings may be added for stations, yards, or industries inside the inner loop without disturbing the high-speed potential of the outer one.

Continued from page 67

you must be selective in planning the scene or activity you intend to model, and you'll have to compress it to fit. That is why many people try to focus on one locale or central theme when building a layout. The kind of operation they enjoy most dictates where the focus will be.

HIGH-SPEED RUNNING

Fast running is a luxury in model railroading because it requires a lot of space. Since such highballing is usually possible only in the open countryside, scenery can be sparse and minimal. If opening the throttle and bending into a curve at 100 miles an hour is your kick, concentrate on a long, well-maintained main line. Don't try to fit it on a 4 x 8 sheet of plywood.

STATION-CENTERED OPERATION

The activity generated around a passenger or freight station is a popular focus for layouts. Trains arrive and depart on schedule. Meanwhile, cars are picked up or dropped at the station yard. These layouts often require interesting traffic manipulation of both freight and passenger trains as they progress through the operation cycle of a typical day.

Although not as severe as with the open countryside layouts, the selective compression of space is important. A full-scale model of a combination freight and passenger station complex in even a modest city would take up more space than most basements have to offer.

YARD AND INDUSTRIAL LAYOUTS

Because of space limitations, these are by far the most common type of layouts. They cram a lot of activity into tight quarters. Switch engines make up trains from cars located on spurs and sidings throughout the layout, then the road locomotive couples on, and the train rolls away. The same scenario can be played out in reverse, with almost infinite variation. Trackside accessories compound the fun. These are busy, "hands-on" layouts that lend themselves well to one or several operators, so family and friends can join in.

Many layout builders try to combine elements from more than one theme, such as a station scene surrounded by loops of track for continuous high-speed running, or a point-to-point railroad with a station at one end and an industrial complex or freight yard at the other. A good plan, formulated in advance, is essential in making the best use of available space.

Begin by looking at a basic track layout book. Several good ones are on the market and are listed in the back of this book. Pick out ideas that fit your available space and desired railroad activity. You can tailor them to suit your tastes and needs.

Putting together and taking apart track sections until you get it right works fine on the living room floor or under the Christmas tree, but this is different.

Planning on paper is the necessary first step in building your permanent model train layout. It provides the valuable opportunity to see how your railroad will look and work before you start construction. If you make a mistake, you can correct it with an eraser instead of a crowbar.

First, make a rough sketch of your space. Take accurate measurements of the overall dimensions. Draw in the size and location of obstacles or limitations that will affect your plan, such as pipes, drains, columns, windows, doors, tanks, and a water heater or furnace.

Next, make an accurate scale drawing of the space with all the obstacles in place on white Bristol board or cardboard. Use heavy ink lines. This will be your basic framework. The scale you use will depend upon the overall size of your space. It should be of workable size, neither too large nor too small (1 inch equals 1 foot is easy and popular). You don't have to be a skillful draftsman; just be as accurate and as neat as you can.

If you have a T-square and triangle, great; however, a plain ruler will do fine. A three-sided architect's scale is handy, but not essential unless you are working in an odd proportion. You'll need a compass for drawing circles, a pen, medium pencils, and a good eraser. Track templates are available to assist you in making accurate drawings. Check with your local hobby shop.

Then tape a large sheet of tracing paper over the framework and make your pencil drawings of track plans on it. This allows you to try many ideas and move things around to see what will fit and what won't. If you make a mistake, simply tape on a fresh sheet of tracing paper and try again. It's easier than drawing a new framework each time you change your mind.

Another advantage to using tracing paper is that you can plan the building of your layout in stages, sections, or steps. The first sheet can show the track plan in the first stage of construction. Then, as growth and expansion are contemplated, these improvements can be shown, step by step, on subsequent overlay sheets. Scenic features, accessories, and buildings can be included on the drawings as they are to be added.

This tracing paper technique gives you a concrete visualization of the layout in its stages. Planning to build your layout in manageable steps is practical. That way you won't have the expense of buying all the track, switches, and accessories at one time. You can start operating sooner and can eliminate the bugs in the first stage before you start on the second.

Various computer software programs are available to assist you in planning your layout. Check with local hobby shops for details. These new programs can eliminate some of the "tracing paper" steps described here, but they are an expensive trade-off unless you are designing a fairly large and sophisticated model railroad.

CLUB AND MODULAR LAYOUTS

For the growing number of people now living in apartments and condominiums, finding enough room to erect a toy train layout can be a serious problem. These compact dwelling units, even the so-called "luxury" ones, are designed for basic functional living and no more. If you want to have space for your hobby, you had better be a stamp collector. This is one of the reason why model railroad clubs and "modular" layouts have become so popular in recent years.

In the traditional model railroad club, each member contributes his time and special talents toward the construction and operation of a shared permanent layout that's located in space owned or rented by the club. Since most clubs have their own workshops, almost all the hobby activity takes place there. Periodic "open house" sessions at the club facilities serve to recruit new members and raise operating funds, thereby keeping membership dues at an affordable level in spite of the high overhead. The club idea has flourished in New York and other cities with large populations of apartment dwellers for more than half a century.

The newest concept in club layouts is a more transitory modular one. Each member is responsible for building and maintaining his own module—a small and independent section of the whole layout, which goes together (and comes apart) like an interlocking jigsaw puzzle. Modular layouts are very portable. They can be set up almost anywhere and have trains running in an hour or two. They don't need space to be permanently housed, although some of them are.

Modular club layouts are the ones often seen at hobby shows and shopping malls. They are the ultimate promotional device and popular attraction, even at events that have little or nothing to do with railroading. Although many modular layouts are stored in club facilities when not in use, they don't have to be. By design, the individual units are usually small enough to be transported in a minivan and slid under a bed.

So just because you live in an apartment or condo, that doesn't mean you can't enjoy the fun of building and operating a layout for your toy trains. The modular concept may be the answer for you. Join a club or, better yet, organize one.

Begin running trains as soon as possible. Get some track in place so
you can see the three-dimensional picture as your layout takes shape.

BUILDING YOUR LAYOUT

TAKE YOUR TIME. Work slowly and carefully. A good portion of the fun is getting there. If you allow your construction to follow the logical steps or stages set forth in your plan, you will avoid the old Roman "one-day nemesis" and the waste that haste often makes. (So much for old saws and platitudes.) Chances are the craftsmanship will be better too.

Allow your layout to expand naturally within the orderly framework of your plan. As you progress with construction, many details will become apparent and ideas will emerge that were not obvious on paper. For example, by moving a siding over just an inch you make room to add a coal loader later. Go with the flow, and never stop experimenting. These little touches will give the finished layout personality.

Start running trains early on. Lay some track so you can see the trains moving through your space. This will give you a three-dimensional perspective on the project that isn't possible from a plan on paper. You may discover, for instance, that those S curves in the yards that looked so symmetrical and artistic on paper cause an inordinate number of derailments. Change them before you go on to the next stage.

BENCHWORK

Scale model railroaders refer to the framework that supports the track and scenery as "benchwork," regardless of the type of construction used. I'll follow suit. There are many ways to build good benchwork for your layout. Your choice will be largely a matter of preference, based upon your track plan and your level of carpentry skill.

Keep two points in mind; they apply to all construction methods. First, make it sturdy. Of course, benchwork should be strong enough to sustain the weight of track, scenery, and trains without bending or buckling. But it's a good idea to reinforce the structure so it will support your own weight as well. Some day you may have to climb up on it to work on something.

Second, make it level. Trains run best on horizontal surfaces. Don't count on your floor being flat or even. Benchwork can be leveled more easily during construction than later on. A few dollars invested in a carpenter's spirit level will pay off in smoother performance down the line. Grades (gentle and not steep) can be fun and make for interesting operational problems, but build them where you want them in your layout, not where they land accidentally.

SIMPLE TRAIN BOARDS OR PLATFORMS

The most popular toy train layout base for over a half century has been a standard 4 x 8-foot sheet of plywood. It is commonly elevated and supported on something: a set of legs, a couple of sawhorses, an old table.

Many fine layouts have been built on multiples of these 4 x 8 platforms that are connected in some way. They provide an excellent beginning because they can be expanded and extended in almost any direction. The examples given in the previous chapter show these handy platforms as modules that can be used as part of a larger layout complex. They contain switching yards, stations, and industrial areas, all of which can be connected by main lines running between them, perhaps on narrow open-grid benchwork.

Because plywood tends to warp and sag, these simple platforms are often framed with 1″ x 4″ lumber underneath. Joists or cross-braces every 2 feet or so provide the necessary rigidity. The pieces are held together with wood screws or with nails and glue.

Less expensive alternatives to plywood are available, with particle board and wafer board being good. The construction methods remain the same. Homasote, which costs about as much as plywood, is lighter but less rigid, so more joists or cross-braces are needed. Whether you choose plywood, Homasote, or the cheaper materials, the boards should be at least half an inch thick.

THE COOKIE CUTTER METHOD

What is popularly known as the "cookie cutter method" is not so much a separate construction method as it is a way of modifying flat tabletop layouts to make them more interesting. Scale model

Modelers often use 4 x 8-foot plywood platforms framed with 1 x 4 lumber as the first step toward building a larger layout.

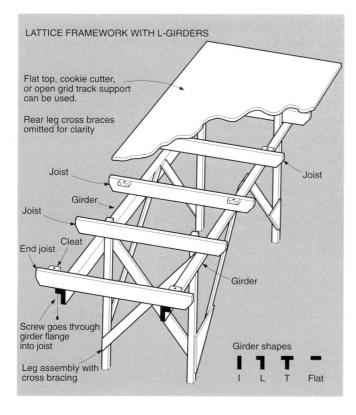

LATTICE FRAMEWORK WITH L-GIRDERS

Flat top, cookie cutter, or open grid track support can be used.

Rear leg cross braces omitted for clarity

Joist

Joist

Girder

Joist

Cleat

End joist

Screw goes through girder flange into joist

Leg assembly with cross bracing

Girder

Girder shapes

I   L   T   Flat

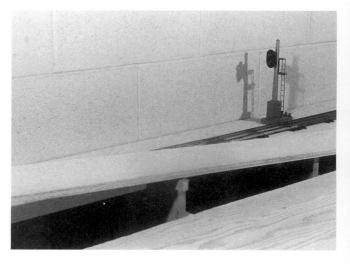

The cookie cutter method is a fine technique for easing into grades. The plywood tabletop is sliced along both sides of the future roadbed and propped up from underneath with risers.

railroaders have long used it to enhance the terrain of their layouts. Scenic features such as hills and mountains can be piled on top of the platform, but what of details like lakes and streams, which normally appear below the level of the surrounding ground?

The answer is provided with the judicious use of a saber saw. Holes for these terrain features can be cut

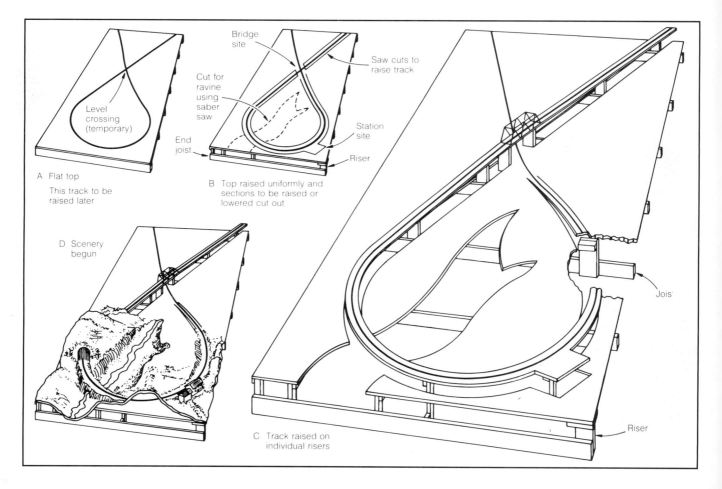

Bridge site

Saw cuts to raise track

Cut for ravine using saber saw

Level crossing (temporary)

Station site

End joist

Riser

A Flat top

This track to be raised later

B Top raised uniformly and sections to be raised or lowered cut out

D Scenery begun

Joist

C Track raised on individual risers

Riser

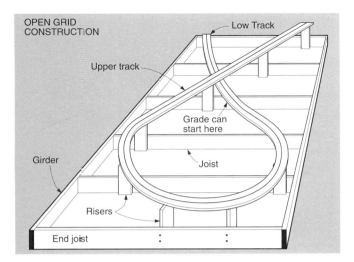

OPEN GRID CONSTRUCTION
Low Track
Upper track
Grade can start here
Joist
Girder
Risers
End joist

into the board at appropriate places, and bottoms for them can be put in later, along with the scenery. These saber saw cuts can be made almost anywhere. Their size and shape are unimportant as long as they don't weaken the overall structure. This is another good

reason for having a well-developed plan before you start to build.

The cookie cutter method also works well if you are planning a layout with different track levels or grades. By slicing the tabletop for several feet along both sides of the roadbed, you can elevate it gradually, thereby easing your track gently into the grade. This method is the best I've seen for minimizing the problems that often occur where the grade begins.

OPEN FRAMEWORK

This system is great for permanent installations. It is by far the most versatile and inexpensive construction method, and the one preferred by many scale model railroaders. It requires more carpentry skill than the tabletop, but not much. If you can handle a hammer, screwdriver, and saw, chances are you will get by.

Open-framework construction provides the most effective means of custom fitting the track plan to the available space. It uses a system of joists, risers, and roadbed over an open L-girder frame. The structure

Open-framework construction is versatile and inexpensive. It is the recommended benchwork for permanent installations.

Open-frame benchwork uses L-girders and risers to support the roadbed.

may be freestanding, attached to a wall, or supported in some other way. There are several different methods of building open-frame benchwork, each having its own application. The one you choose depends on your individual needs and situation. Pick up a copy of *How to Build Model Railroad Benchwork,* 2nd edition, by Linn H. Westcott and Rick Selby (Kalmbach Publishing Co., 1996). This book is must reading before you begin. It provides step-by-step instructions and will help you avoid serious pitfalls.

Open framework, because of its versatility, provides the ideal base for sophisticated scenery.

LAYING YOUR TRACK

O N MOST LAYOUTS, the track is fastened to the benchwork. Almost since the beginning, toy train manufacturers have recommended this practice, stressing the desirability of erecting permanent settings for their products. Although they made sectional track, they put holes in the cross-ties so nails, screws, or bolts could be easily inserted. This undoubtedly was done to counteract the natural tendencies of tinplate track to come apart at the joints and to "wander" across the floor.

You will probably use one of the following traditional methods of laying your track, unless you are like a friend of mine. He enjoys designing new layouts and thinks much of the fun with trains is found in putting together and taking apart the track. In the center of his train room, he built an elevated, carpet-covered, 6 x 10-foot layout "bed."

Nothing is permanently attached or even normally placed on this odd-looking, sacrosanct structure. It sticks up like a green mesa or ancient Indian burial mound amid the more conventional decor. Whenever he gets the urge to run trains from his ample collection, he starts from scratch, setting up the track and accessories, connecting the wires, and putting the trains on the track. He says that having a new layout each time he operates his trains keeps him from getting bored.

TRACK TIPS

New vs. used sectional track. Whether you decide to buy new track for your layout or recondition used sections will make little operational difference. The only real argument for new track is appearance. It will depend upon your priorities and the layout you want. Used track can generally be found in quantity at swap meets and hobby shops for a fraction of the price of new. So the trade-off pits money against time and effort.

Reconditioning old track. When buying used track, examine each section carefully. Avoid bundles and boxed lots. Be sure the rails are straight and the third-rail insulators are all in place. You will need three pins for each section. While these are available separately, they are expensive that way.

Remove any dirt and grime by soaking the track in a strong solution of laundry detergent and warm water for about 15 minutes (laundry tubs are great for this). Then scrub each section with a stiff-bristled brush and rinse under the tap. Let the track air-dry. In many cases this is all the cleaning that will be required.

New and used sectional track is widely available.

When the track has dried, check each section to be sure all pins are tight. If necessary, crimp the holes on the opposite ends with needlenose pliers to ensure a tight fit.

Rust can be removed with sandpaper or a wire wheel mounted in an electric drill. Nonmetallic kitchen scouring pads work well too, but never use steel wool on track. Small particles tend to stick to the rails until they are picked up by a locomotive's Magne-Traction. It doesn't take many of those particles to gum up the works.

The top running surfaces of the rails are most important for good operation. They must be free of dirt, oxide, and rust. Some people finish treating their track by rubbing it with WD-40 on a cloth. This is optional.

LAYING TRACK

Fit sections together snugly. A tight fit between the sections is essential for good electrical conductivity. Loose pins waste precious energy. Sections not joined fully cause unwanted bumps as trains pass over. Smooth operation begins with carefully laid track.

Lay it straight. Use a straightedge if possible to ensure that straight track runs do not have unsightly kinks. A yardstick is handy for this. Then eyeball the rails just to make sure.

Fasten it securely. The trick is to use just enough pressure when fastening the track. Too much will bend the cross-ties and distort the profile of the rails, and too little will allow for unwanted lateral play.

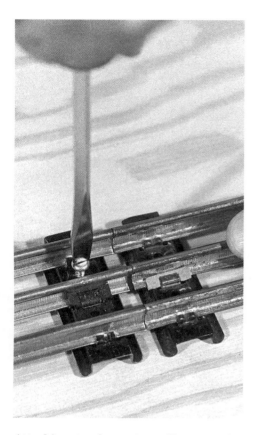

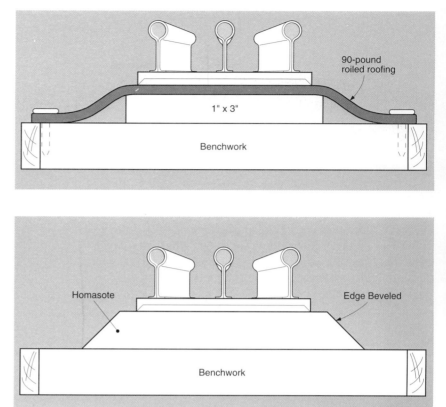

Attaching track sections direct to the tabletop is not difficult. All you need are a screwdriver and some screws.

Two examples of roadbed cross-sections. A traditional approach was to use roofing to shape the contour; a more current approach is to cut or buy roadbed already shaped.

Whether you use screws or nails is only a matter of preference or convenience. Using nails to hold the track down is faster, but be careful to hit only the nails and not the rails. Screws give you better control of the holding pressure and are easier to remove if you should change your mind. Screws seem to be the hands-down choice of most hobbyists.

The number and size of the screws depend on the base material of your benchwork or roadbed. One or two screws per section is adequate for plywood and hardboards. Softer bases, such as Homasote, require a minimum of three per section. I recommend drilling guide holes in the harder substances before inserting the screws (½" x 3 for O-27 track and ¾" x 4 for O gauge).

ROADBED

Whether you use roadbed under your track is also a matter of choice. The type of roadbed will be determined by your budget. There is a wide range of available options, from commercially prepared cork or rubber roadbed to the home-brew variety made from Homasote or wood.

The most common "non-roadbed" method of securing track sections is driving screws or nails to attach it direct to the benchwork or tabletop. This gives the effect of the old New York Central's Water Level

Route—flat. The benchwork is usually though not always painted or treated first.

Some collectors, who are more interested in building a working display for their prized items than a lifelike model railroad, simply carpet their train boards with the green indoor-outdoor stuff and lay their track right on top of it.

In the old days, before commercial products were available, many modelers used common 1 x 3 lumber for their roadbeds. Over it they stretched long strips of gray or brown rolled roofing material. The coarse grain of the pebbled roofing gave the impression of ballast.

Lumber and roofing material is still a good way to have roadbed at a reasonable price. The lumber sells for pennies per foot, and the roofing comes in 90-pound rolls that are 3 feet wide. (There will be enough for your railroad as well as a toolshed or chicken coop.) Check with roofing contractors and building supply companies; they often have remnants for sale cheap. Of course, the curves will have to be cut and spliced from the straight lumber, but that's part of the fun.

If you have the right equipment, you can saw sheets of Homasote or half-inch plywood to the correct size to form your roadbed. This method is popular among scale model railroaders. Curves and beveled edges are no problem, if you have the skill and the proper saws. If not, read on.

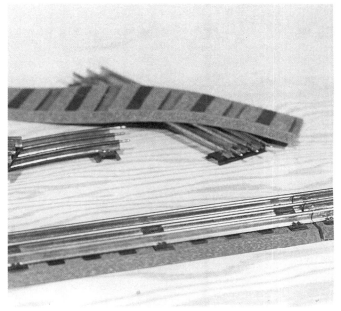

Left: Commercial cork roadbed installed under conventional Lionel track. Right: Commercial rubber roadbed can be nailed, screwed, or glued to the benchwork.

Commercial cork roadbed can be used with any type of track, including GarGraves sections.

Although sold under a number of trade names, prepared, commercial roadbeds are made from only three basic materials, rubber, cork, or Homasote.

The rubber roadbed simulates the kind that Lionel and others used to sell for use with their toy trains. Basically, the track sections fit into the roadbed sections, thereby swallowing up the formed sheet-metal cross-ties and giving the track a sleek and finished look. The ones I've seen were made of gray rubber, with simulated black cross-ties painted on. Nails or screws can be driven through this roadbed in the conventional manner, or it can be glued to the benchwork.

Designed mainly for scale model railroads, cork roadbed is available in several thicknesses and works

Inserting additional wood ties under conventional Lionel tinplate track improves its appearance.

fine with tinplate or the more realistic GarGraves three-rail track. It, too, can be glued to the benchwork or attached with small nails. The track is most often then screwed through the roadbed and into the benchwork below. For this you need slightly longer screws. Because the cork is resilient, be careful not to drive in the screws too far.

Prepared roadbed made from Homasote is also available. It comes in curvable 3-foot sections with neatly beveled edges. Like the others, it is easy to use and can be nailed, screwed, or glued in place.

Regardless of the roadbed you use, sectional tinplate track can be dressed up to look more realistic by inserting extra wood ties between the sheet-metal ones. These can be made by sawing wood into the same dimensions as the metal ties, then dipping them into dark gray stain. Placing four wood ties between each pair of sheet-metal ones will look right.

One of the great advantages of using Homasote, cork, or rubber roadbed is the inherent sound-absorbing quality of these materials. They can act as insulation between the rails and the benchwork, thus reducing operating noise significantly. Be sure to install them correctly. There can be no contact, either direct or through nails or screws, between the track and the large wooden structure supporting the layout.

With rubber roadbed, installation is simple. Just glue the roadbed to the benchwork. That's all there is to it.

The silencing qualities of cork roadbed are about the same as rubber. Gluing it to the benchwork is recommended. Most of it is too thin to use anything but glue on the track side as well, which creates a problem with conventional tinplate track sections. There just isn't enough surface under the ties for glue to hold them securely. Therefore, cork roadbed is only workable if you use track that has many flat wood ties, such as GarGraves.

Homasote is thick enough to be used successfully with almost any kind of track. It isn't, however, as soft and sound-absorbent as cork or rubber. It can be glued or screwed to the benchwork. If you use flathead screws to hold the Homasote in place, countersink the holes so that the screwheads are beneath the surface level of the roadbed. Make sure the screws holding the track are short enough that they don't go through the Homasote and into the benchwork. Use three per section for a solid hold.

By the way, painting these sound-deadening roadbeds hinders their absorbency and curtails their effectiveness.

INSULATED TRACK SECTIONS

If you plan ahead, you can substitute insulated track sections for those bothersome and unsightly pressure contactors to operate trackside accessories. Nothing spoils the effect of a tight, well-constructed layout quicker than seeing long stretches of track bob up and down as a train passes over them. Such floating sections are needed to activate crossing gates, signals, lights, gatemen, and the like in the conventional way. And the contactors need constant adjustment.

As you lay your track, install insulated sections wherever you would normally use a single-pole, single-throw contactor, such as Lionel's 145-C. These insulated sections can be as long as you wish. (This is particularly effective with crossing gates, since they can be made to go down before the train arrives.) Insulated sections are reliable and never slip out of adjustment. Furthermore, because the weight of the train is not a factor, all track sections can be fastened tightly to the roadbed.

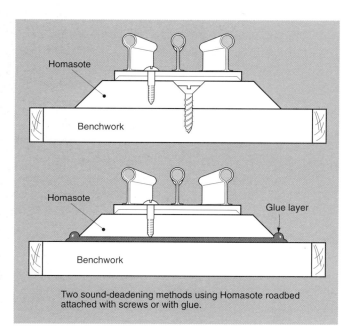

Two sound-deadening methods using Homasote roadbed attached with screws or with glue.

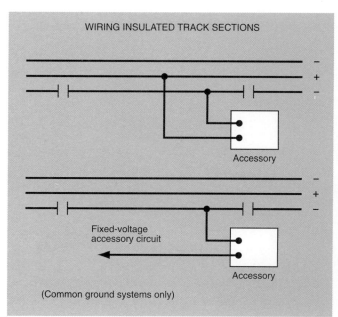

WIRING INSULATED TRACK SECTIONS

(Common ground systems only)

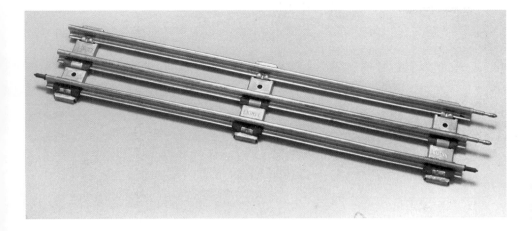

This finished insulated track section is ready to install on a layout.

Instead of using pressure caused by the weight of the passing train, the metal wheels and axles of the train itself complete the electrical circuit to operate the accessory. This is accomplished by insulating one of the running rails of the track section. It's really simple.

You can buy such special track sections or make your own. In addition to the section to be insulated, you will need the three fiber insulators from the third rail of a discarded track section and two plastic insulating track pins from your hobby dealer.

First, remove either of the running rails from the track section. With a screwdriver, pry the metal "fin-gers" on each tie until the rail comes loose. Next, insert the plastic insulating pins into both ends of this rail. Then position the three fiber insulators on it in the appropriate places.

Then replace the rail and crimp it in the cross-ties. Make sure the fiber insulators are properly centered in each cross-tie and you haven't accidentally broken through them when crimping the rail.

The two wires leading to the accessory can then be connected to the insulated running rail and to the third rail of the track, or to your fixed-voltage accessory circuit, if you have one. (See the next chapter about these special circuits.)

David Dansky displays his outstanding collection along the walls of a rather overwhelming room he calls a "personal fantasy land." In the center he has built a beautiful multiple-gauge layout on which he can run his trains, all of which are intended to operate.

PHOTO GALLERY
DISPLAYS AND LAYOUTS

VISITING THE DISPLAYS and layouts of other toy train enthusiasts is one of the joys of this hobby. It's exciting and informative to see what other people have collected and how they showcase them. An invitation to the home of another hobbyist can expand your horizons as you view pieces that you had only heard about. You may pick up ideas about how to show off your trains and which items you'll want to search for.

As the photographs in this section make clear, some enthusiasts prefer to place their trains on shelves or in glass cases. They like to sit and admire the beauty and colors of the models they have collected. Doing so can be relaxing after a hard day at work,

especially if looking at the trains triggers memories of childhood or recent hunts at train shows.

Other hobbyists can't imagine letting their models sit still as dust gathers on them. Instead, they plan and build layouts on which their S, O, or Standard gauge trains and accessories are operated, just as the families did that originally owned them. Watching locomotives speed across track and reliable accessories again load materials, illuminate a room, or control a train's movement reminds us of why vintage toy trains mean so much to us. Whichever approach appeals most to you, the thrills and pleasures of this hobby will become apparent as you enjoy the pictures in this section.

One of the most wonderful things about toy train displays is that they're so colorful. Joey D'Angelo's collection includes fine examples of brightly colored locomotives and motorized units. Not all collectors have their trains so elegantly displayed, but most like to show off their acquisitions.

Bill Kraemer artistically blends scale and toy trains and accessories
into the scenery on his O gauge hi-rail model railroad.

As shown by Vance Kinlaw's S gauge layout, effective scenery combines the natural and the artificial in a way that seems logical and convincing.

The legacy of pioneer toy train collector LaRue Shempp is on display in the Lycoming County Historical Museum at Williamsport, Pennsylvania. Two rare American Flyer sets are shown on the glass case in the foreground.

Grandstand displays such as this were popular in department stores back in the 1940s and '50s. Ed Dougherty built this one to show his Lionel F3 and GG1 passenger sets.

Glass cases like this one can be used to highlight certain interesting facets of a collection. Richard Kughn uses a showcase to display his Lionel illuminated houses from the early 1930s.

Richard Kughn, former owner of Lionel Trains Inc. during the late 1980s through mid-1990s, has a tremendous Lionel Standard gauge layout in a facility he calls "Carail." The structure houses much of his classic automobile collection as well as his train collection and several layouts. This wonderful Standard gauge kingdom is about as big as it gets!

Passenger station activity on three levels catches the attention of visitors to Steve Bales's O gauge layout.

Men who had toy trains as boys in the 1950s often gravitated to HO scale in the 1960s and '70s. As they got older, they remembered the trains of their youth and returned to O gauge, putting to use the track planning and scenery techniques they leared as scale modelers. Now, at the turn of the century, they're known as "hi-railers." This photo was taken on Ira Butler, Jr.'s layout.

A portion of Tom Frye's extensive collection of American Flyer S gauge trains and accessories. He displays his favorite pieces in this section.

This section of the collection of Chris Gans shows its eclectic nature. Lionel Standard gauge freight cars have been placed next to O gauge streamliners and scarce O gauge trains from European manufacturers.

The late Frank Sinatra was idolized by millions for his smooth singing style. Toy train fans remember him as much for his love of Lionel trains, however, and feel a sense of fraternity with him. Ol' Blue Eyes, we're told, spent hours in his custom-built train room just watching the trains run. That fascination is certainly not limited to celebrities.

Railroading through the open countryside on Seth Giem's O gauge railroad. Plenty of room for the engineer to open the throttle.

Brad Nelson planned a bustling industrial area for his S gauge layout.

WIRING YOUR LAYOUT

IN THE DAYS before the federal government's venture into consumer protectionism, Lionel, Gilbert, and other firms manufactured large, all-in-one transformers to power toy train layouts. The Lionel ZW was rated at 275 watts and the deluxe Gilbert unit at 350. Both were capable of handling an entire layout—two or three trains plus trackside lights and accessories. Having several independent circuits, they were convenient and easy to hook up. The controls were all up-front and at hand.

The super power provided by these transformers was enough to run the biggest locomotives and the longest trains with plenty of energy in reserve to overcome the losses inherent in large track spreads. Of course, these products were reflective of an age that worshipped power. Long, sleek automobiles with 400 cube V-8 engines that guzzled 100-octane ethyl gas and could go 120 mph flat out were the national norm.

In the early 1970s, the same bureaucrats who insisted on childproof caps for patent medicine bottles declared these mammoth transformers unsafe for use by little humans. Although there had been no reported cases of electrocution by ZW, the potential shock hazard, if the transformers were improperly used by infants or idiots, was enough to set these functionaries to worrying about protecting the future electorate.

They didn't care whether your train slowed to a crawl every time you tried to blow the whistle any more than they cared that you couldn't get the cap off your aspirin bottle in the middle of the night. Their job was to preserve the republic. As a result, today's train transformers, like today's automobile engines, are sorry compromises between what is technologically possible and what is socially and politically expedient.

POWER SOURCES

When choosing the right power source for your layout, you basically have four options:

• If you're lucky, you may find an old high-wattage transformer that still performs according to specifications. Since replacement parts are available, many of these giants are reconditioned and offered for sale by used toy train dealers. But demand has driven up their prices, so you can expect to pay a premium, particularly for highly desirable and well-built units such as the Lionel ZW. Many hobbyists consider these old warhorses to be the best for operating layouts, regardless of price. If you decide to use an old transformer, first have it thoroughly inspected and tested by a qualified service technician.

• A number of new solid-state electronic units that were designed as replacements for the outlawed high-wattage standard transformers have been on the market for years. This entire line of products gained a bad reputation initially because some of the early ones were poorly designed and performed unreliably. The

Powerful toy train transformers from the 1960s.

Basic components of the new Lionel TrainMaster control system, which uses state-of-the-art electronic technology to operate toy trains. The handheld, walkaround control uses radio frequencies to communicate commands to the other components, thus eliminating wires between the operator and the layout.

their specifications can be confusing to people accustomed to thinking in terms of plain old watts and volts.

• On the next logical step up the scale from simple electronic transformer substitutes are the new control systems using computer technology. Several different brands are currently on the market. All of them allow for sophisticated control options as well as the operation of the sound systems built into the latest high-end hi-rail locomotives. Each of these brands features some form of handheld, walkaround throttle capabilities.

Although it is beyond the scope of this book to delve into the comparative features and relative merits of the available systems, it is fair to indicate that they are all budget busters and are not necessarily compatible. So, do some research and discuss your needs with a hobby dealer before you decide to purchase one of these systems. Of course, if you must have the latest, up-to-the-minute technological toys (in addition to your toy trains), enjoy realistic sound effects, and are comfortable running your trains with a key pad instead of a transformer handle, then one of these new system just may be right for you.

• This alternative may well be the most practical. Use a battery of smaller transformers instead of one large unit. This system works quite well on small- to medium-sized layouts that are divided into "blocks," or zones of independent control. Each block has its own transformer to control the train running within it. This gives each block independent speed and reversing control, which is a bonus. Since only one train at a time should be in any given block, the system works. Additional separate transformers, as many as needed, can be used for accessory and lighting circuits.

This type of small transformer hookup is the most economical option. At least it will work until alternative power sources are acquired. Who knows? You may like it well enough to keep it and spend your train money for other things. Old 60-, 75-, or 100-watt transformers will run almost any train over a relatively short stretch of track. Both Lionel and Gilbert made

flaws have long since been corrected, and today's models are undoubtedly better; however, they are still a compromise. They work, but not as well as they might under all conditions, particularly when compared to conventional transformers. And they aren't cheap. While I won't comment or differentiate among the various types and brands, I will advise caution when making your selection. Some of the terminology used in

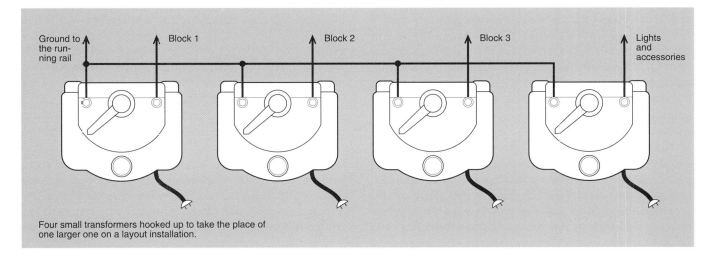

Four small transformers hooked up to take the place of one larger one on a layout installation.

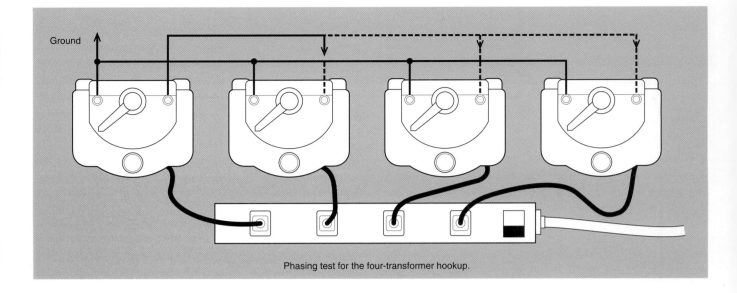

Phasing test for the four-transformer hookup.

them by the millions, so they may be had at most swap meets for very reasonable prices. This is all you really need for basic operation.

To use several transformers in this way, they must be put in phase with each other and share a common-ground connection. Common-ground wiring is recommended no matter what power source you choose. It is detailed on the next page. The phasing operation is easy and has to be carried out only once.

PHASING TRANSFORMERS

Whenever you use two or more transformers in an installation, they should be put into phase with each other to ensure smooth operation. This simply means wiring each one to the layout in the same way and plugging all the line cords into the outlets in the same way each time. To make it easy to understand, one terminal on each transformer will be designated as "hot" (+) and the other as "ground" (-). The hot leads will eventually be connected to the inside third rails of the track. The ground will go to the outside running rails.

First, all the ground terminals on the transformer should be connected with heavy wire. Most of the larger transformers and some of the smaller ones have a designated ground terminal. (On Lionel products, it's usually labeled "U"; on Gilbert items, it's generally labeled "Base Post.") If your transformer has a designated ground terminal, use it. If not, you may arbitrarily pick one of the two as your own designated ground. It doesn't matter which you choose, but be consistent after that.

Second, plug in all the transformers and turn their speed controls up full. Connect a wire to the hot terminal on the first transformer. Touch it to the hot terminal on the second transformer. If you get a spark, the transformers are not in phase with each other. Reverse the plug on the second transformer. That will

put it in phase with the first. Touch the terminal again. There should be no spark.

Repeat this procedure with all the transformers in your lineup. Then mark the plugs with a notch or a dot of paint so they can be inserted into the outlet in the same way each time. (A multiple outlet bar or strip, particularly one with a master switch, is a wise investment if you plan to use several transformers. That way you can simply use the switch instead of unplugging the transformers each time you suspend operations.)

COMMON GROUND

By using a common ground (some hobbyists call it a "common return") on your layout, you can simplify the wiring and save money. You will need to buy only about half as much wire. Once you understand the theory, you will see that it is the most logical method to use.

There are two things to remember. First, a ground is a ground is a ground, no matter what. Second, electricity is smart. It will always find the most direct path "home," regardless of the traffic. More theory you need not understand. Simple enough?

Scale model railroaders have been using the common-ground principle for years, and the concept is not foreign to the toy train field. Larger transformers—those with several control circuits—usually have internal common grounds. In the multiple-transformer hookup discussed above, the ground terminals are all wired together "in common" with each other.

In the most basic terms, one ground connection may be used for all the blocks in your track system and all of your lights and accessories. That means in the case of track blocks, you need to run only one wire to the hot third rail in each block. The ground is common and continuous through the running rails. For lights and accessories, only the hot wire need be connected to the transformer. The ground, or return wire, can be

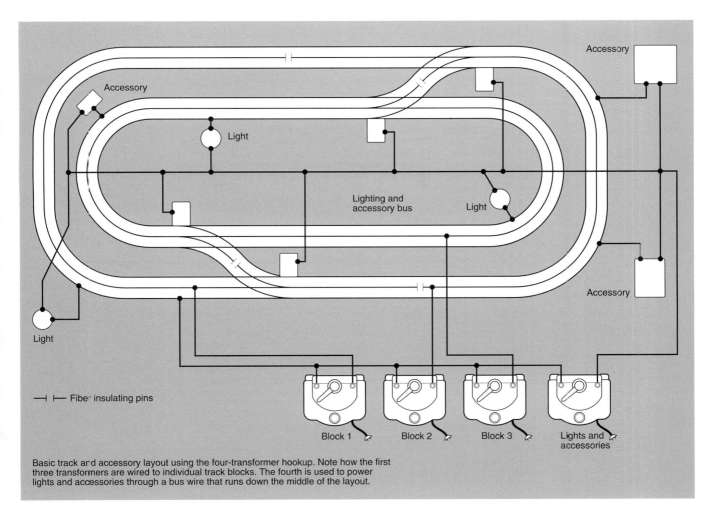

Basic track and accessory layout using the four-transformer hookup. Note how the first three transformers are wired to individual track blocks. The fourth is used to power lights and accessories through a bus wire that runs down the middle of the layout.

attached to the nearest common-ground point. This is often one of the running rails or a special "ground bus," which many hobbyists find effective on larger layouts.

BUS ON A TRAIN LAYOUT?

It's an electrician's term; don't blame me. Bus wires usually run around the periphery of a layout or cut across it diagonally. Their purpose is to provide convenient points to attach lead wires from lights or accessories without having to string wires from each one all the way to the transformer. Some layouts have several buses, one for the common ground, one for switch machines, one for operating accessories, and one for house and streetlights. I highly recommend using a system of these bus wires under your layout, particularly if it includes lots of lights and accessories. Buses can make your wiring easier and neater too.

TWO CONCLUDING SUGGESTIONS

Make all of your connections as simple as possible. For one reason or another, many layout builders tend toward overly complicated wiring schemes. Always use the most direct route and avoid wire "rat's nests" (excessive number of tangled wires) at all costs. Remember, someday you may have to get in there to fix something!

Use heavy enough wire. (Throw away those skinny wires packed with your train set.) The idea is to try to prevent as much current loss as possible in the wiring. Use 12- or 14-gauge wire for buses. Sixteen gauge is the minimum for track feeders. Eighteen- or 20-gauge leads are acceptable for short runs to lights or accessories. Solder connections wherever you can. The resulting smoother operation of your layout will be worth the extra effort and expenditure.

More specific wiring details are beyond the scope of this work. For greater depth on this subject I recommend Peter H. Riddle's three-volume set on *Wiring Your Lionel Layout* (available from Kalmbach Publishing Co.). These excellent books take you from primary concepts all the way through advanced and sophisticated techniques.

Model railroad scenery can be almost as breathtaking as that in real life, as Robert Yanosey proves on his O gauge layout.

ADDING SCENERY

TRYING TO CRAM as much operation as possible into every inch of your layout space can be tempting, but it leads you into a trap when the time comes to install scenery. The goal is to make your layout look as though the scenery was there first and the railroad came later. So it is essential that you plan your scenery as carefully as you plan your track layout.

Real railroads have a purpose, a reason for being where they are—a community to serve, industrial or agricultural freight to haul, passengers to carry. Model ones should have a purpose, too. If you ignore this point and don't allow room for the scenery that provides a logical environment in which your trains can function, you won't have a model railroad at all. Instead, you'll have just a bunch of tracks on a board.

Of course, if you like a bunch of tracks on a board, that's fine. Just ignore this chapter.

MAN AGAINST NATURE

Mother Nature may be law-abiding, but she is also highly irregular and unpredictable. She thrives on infinite variation—no two rocks or snowflakes are alike. No flat surfaces, perfect circles, right angles, or straight lines mark the natural geographic environment. People, on the other hand, are more inclined toward uniformity and geometry in the structures they create.

Effective layout scenery combines these two, but in a backwards way. Instead of putting the geometrical or uniform human fabrications into the geographical and irregular terrain, as in the real world, we have to build the geographical around the geometrical and try to make it seem logical and believable. Perhaps this is what scares many hobbyists away from constructing scenery.

This scene on Roger Casanova's O gauge layout uses different levels of track and a painted backdrop to give the illusion of depth and space.

SPECIAL SKILLS NOT REQUIRED

We are all so accustomed to thinking in terms of designing geometrical shapes, even in our arts and crafts, that if we don't have a certain amount of dexterity at it, we tend to give up before we begin. We are intimidated into believing that unless we have training in art, masonry, or carpentry, we have no business tackling toy train scenery.

Nothing could be further from the truth. It may actually be beneficial to be a ten-thumbed klutz, because those "aberrations" you normally inflict upon the world of the geometrical will look spectacular in the world of the geographical. You can't make a mistake when modeling nature—a prototype can always be found somewhere. So you have no excuse to neglect building scenery on your layout.

ANY KID CAN DO IT!

The basic techniques of constructing scenery are familiar to most children, if they have ever made papier-mâché masks in school or sand castles at the beach. These are messy, hands-on operations that kids love.

That may be another reason adults sometimes shy away. So let the youngsters help. Many families have found this to be an excellent place to involve the kids, giving them a sense of having made a real contribution to the layout project.

TERMINOLOGY AND MATERIALS

Don't be snowed by the terms often bandied about by those modelers who specialize in scenic effects. All of those technical-sounding terms, such as "hardshell," "softshell," "zip-texturing," and the like actually describe simple processes. Worry about them when and if you ever need them.

The same goes for the materials, many of which have ominous names that conjure up images of exotic and hazardous chemicals. "Gypsum," "epoxy resin," "dolomite," "lichen," "glycerin," "vermiculite," "polymer," and "wet water": all of these are as harmless and almost as common (in the right stores) as latex paint and white glue.

Shop around a bit before you begin. Check local hobby and craft stores. Look in the pages of your favorite model magazines for ideas. Many excellent products are on the market to help you, including a variety of scenery kits. And don't overlook the lumber, hardware, and building supply retailers. They can often provide the materials you'll need in bulk quantities.

DESIGNING TERRAIN FEATURES

Ideally, the terrain on your layout should roll and slope, with the larger scenic features on slightly different levels than the railroad right-of-way. This not only imitates the real world, it creates a more interesting three-dimensional picture. Open-frame benchwork lends itself well to this kind of treatment. Hills, valleys, cuts, and fills can be formed easily by raising or lowering the scenery supports.

Although you may have a more difficult time achieving this on a tabletop layout, it certainly isn't impossible. Grades and hills can be built right on top of the flat surface. Depressions in the landscape can be made using the cookie cutter method, sawing out sections of the tabletop and installing a false bottom below track level. If you are clever, you can even go from one to the other by sloping the terrain smoothly.

Above the surface. One hill in isolation will look out of place, so make several of varying sizes and shapes that are connected in some way. A rolling slope of earth leading up gradually from track level to the major hills is best. This continuity in your landscaping will keep your hills from looking like so many islands, swimming in a tabletop sea. Cuts can be effective, particularly if your track passes through them.

Below the surface. Sections of a tabletop can be removed using a saber saw to make way for ponds, streams, ditches, or other terrain features usually found below track level. When doing this, be careful not to cut away important braces or supports, thus weakening your benchwork. False bottoms can be attached or built under the table surface.

To simulate water in a pond or stream, install a sheet of glass or Plexiglas tinted blue-green over a below-the-surface riverbed or pond bottom. Features such as rocks and weeds on the bottom will be visible through the glass. Paint the bottom of the pond in a light earth tone and blend in darker shades for an uneven appearance, which will look more realistic.

Adding a few hills and mounds above the table surface and a couple of features below track level will create the illusion that your layout is not a flattop one, even if it is.

GONNA BUILD A MOUNTAIN

Well, would you believe a hill? Consider this to be an experiment or a demonstration to show how easy and enjoyable it can be. We will use only common materials, many of which you probably have around the house:

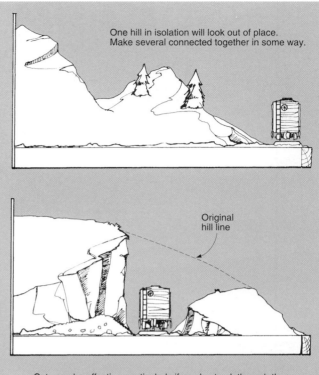

One hill in isolation will look out of place. Make several connected together in some way.

Original hill line

Cuts can be effective, particularly if you lay track through them.

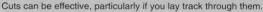

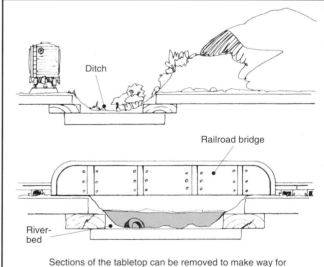

Ditch

Railroad bridge

Riverbed

Sections of the tabletop can be removed to make way for terrain features usually found below track level.

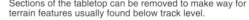

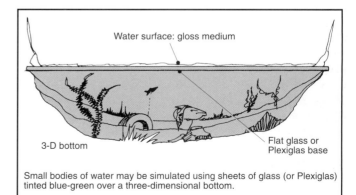

Water surface: gloss medium

3-D bottom

Flat glass or Plexiglas base

Small bodies of water may be simulated using sheets of glass (or Plexiglas) tinted blue-green over a three-dimensional bottom.

98

First, position the newspaper wads in the general contour you want and lay strips of masking tape over them to hold them in place.

Plaster of paris (one or two small boxes). If you wish, substitute Hydrocal for the plaster. It is used in the same way and will result in a harder scenery shell. This product is not available everywhere. Check with your lumber and building materials outlets.

Paper towels (one or two rolls)
Old newspapers
Water (from the tap)
Tacks or staples (and something to drive them in)
Masking tape (small roll, about an inch wide)
Old plastic bucket (ice cream pails work well)
Stirring stick

Ready? Start with the newspapers. Separate the pages. Pretend you disagree violently with the political position of the paper. Rip the news and editorial section into shreds—big ones, small ones, long ones, square ones—and wad them up. Then make like you just lost $100 on yesterday's game and take the entire sports section and crumple it, throw it on the floor, and stomp on it a few times. Do the same with the classified ads, but save the funnies. You'll need something to read while the plaster sets.

Position the wadded and crumpled newspapers on the table exactly where you want to build your mountain. Put the large sports and classified wads in the middle and poke the smaller news and editorial wads

around them. When you are satisfied with the contours of your mountain, lay strips of masking tape loosely over the pile of wads to keep them all in place. Then tack or staple the ones around the edges to the tabletop.

Cover your track and everything else in the vicinity with sheets of newspaper that you secure with masking tape. The next operation gets messy.

Cut the roll of paper towels in half with a sharp knife (serrated ones work best). Now you have two rolls of towels that are just the right size. Tear all the towels off the roll and stack them up. You'll have to move swiftly when you start using them.

Measure two cups of cold water into the bucket. Add two cups of plaster and stir the mixture with the stick until it is blended. From this point you have about five minutes until the plaster starts to set. (You can retard the setting time by adding about a tablespoon of vinegar to the water, but it won't give you more than another minute or two.)

One by one, dip the paper towels into the plaster mixture, saturating them. Then lay each one over the wadded newspaper base. Overlap the towels in such a way that there are at least two thicknesses everywhere. More won't hurt.

If you aren't satisfied with the way your mountain is taking shape, wad up more newspaper, poke it into

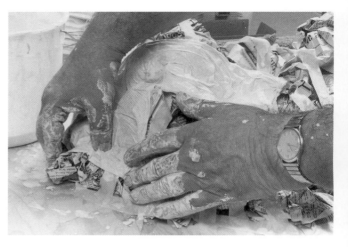

One by one, dip paper towels into the plaster and water mixture. Then lay them over the wadded newspaper.

place, and cover it with the plaster-soaked towels. Ad-libbing juts and crevasses as you go along can be fun—just don't get carried away.

When you have finished laying paper and before the plaster has hardened, wet your hands with plain water and gently smooth out the surface of your mountain. Run your fingers along all the joints between the towels to make sure there are no gaps, cracks, or wrinkles. If necessary, you can apply more plaster-soaked towels over trouble spots. Pay particular attention to the surfaces where the mountain meets the tabletop. A bridge of towels should make the joint imperceptible.

The same techniques can be used on open-frame benchwork as well. Instead of piling wads of newspaper on the tabletop, form hill contours with wooden uprights nailed direct to the benchwork joists. Over these, string a lattice of 1″-wide corrugated cardboard strips or chicken wire (some people have even used masking tape). Next, drape pieces of wet newspaper over the latticework and shape appropriately. When this has dried, apply the plaster-soaked paper towels as above. Three layers of towels are needed in most cases.

In a few days, when the plaster has dried thoroughly, give your mountain two coats of flat latex paint

After you have at least two thicknesses of paper towels everywhere, dribble the remaining plaster and water mixture over the entire structure. Then let it dry for at least 24 hours.

Left: Apply a liberal coat of flat latex paint in your favorite earth tone.
Right: After the first coat has dried, apply a second one. While that is
still wet, sprinkle an artificial grass mixture over the mountain. You
can add ground foam to simulate bushes and weeds.

in the tan or light brown shade of your choice to simulate bare earth. While the second coat is wet, flock the terrain with ground foam in several shades of green and yellow to resemble grassy patches. Your hobby shop or mail-order model supply house can provide ground foam in a variety of colors.

Chances are that business has other scenic details, such as bushes, trees, and rocks, that will add the finishing touches to your project. Or you can make your own using twigs and stones from the backyard.

In addition to the natural scenery, your railroad layout needs evidence of human habitation—buildings, automobiles, and the clutter of civilization. Don't overlook the population itself. Again, your hobby dealer can be helpful with building kits, model motor vehicles, and human and animal figures in the appropriate scale for the little world you have created.

For more in-depth information, I suggest consulting Dave Frary's *Realistic Scenery for Toy Train Layouts,* which is available from Kalmbach.

A Look Toward the Future and a Personal Memoir

THERE HAS NEVER been a better time to get into the toy train hobby. No matter what your preference may be—collecting or operating with new or used equipment—supplies are plentiful and prices fairly stable.

The quality of today's train products is higher than ever. New and innovative electronic technologies provide another dimension of ease and sophistication that makes audio systems play back digitally recorded echoes of the real thing—whistles, bells, steam and diesel sound effects—all synchronized to the movements of the train. Paint jobs are accurately prototypical, and the detailing on some of the better models rivals that of museum pieces. Hi-railers never had it so good.

While the price tags on much of the new merchandise may seem high, you get what you pay for. Price levels are not really out of line, considering the quality of the models. Vigorous competition among toy train manufacturers in recent years has kept them from escalating through the roof, as the prices of used "collectible" trains did a decade or so ago.

On that subject, strong evidence suggests that the collectible toy train market has leveled off. The steep upward price spiral of the 1980s—when waves of baby boomers entered the hobby in search of nostalgic reminders of childhood in postwar America—has peaked out. Some used train prices have actually come down. More will probably follow suit as supply and demand come into equilibrium.

The hobby, in all of its many facets, is strong and healthy overall. So this is a fine time to acquire toy trains for your collection or to run on your layout, but not to use as hedges against inflation or as investments. Those days, if they ever existed, are gone.

Just as the differences between scale and toy trains have diminished (scale being less craft-oriented and toy more realistic), so too will toy train hobbyists of the future probably not make as many distinctions between "collecting" and "operating." Many operators also collect, and collectors are building layouts on which to run their favorite pieces already. This happy combination will undoubtedly continue.

Will the collectors of the future be more or less specialized? Probably less, but that's a hard one to call. Up to a point, it depends upon the supply of goods in relation to the supply of money. Right now, both are plentiful, which encourages diversity. Peer pressure has also been a significant determinant in specialization—people of the same age tend to collect the same kinds of trains. This also may change as the nostalgic element becomes less meaningful and people search for other gratifications from their collections. Except for the very wealthy and the old die-hards, as the supply diminishes over time, there will be less emphasis on having only pristine originals in collections.

The trend toward accepting authentic restorations, reproductions, and even representations has already started. We also can look for more recycling of operating rolling stock, superdetailing, and kitbashing, as hi-railers borrow ideas from the scale model railroaders.

THE HI-RAIL ADVANTAGE

Hi-railing, using toy trains and accessories in a scale-like setting that is complete with buildings, scenery, and all the trimmings, seems to be the wave of the future. As this type of model railroad gained acceptability among adults, a number of the old myths were submerged in the wake of accruing benefits.

Space conservation. The notion that smaller gauges, such as HO, are more space-efficient than O was the last great myth to bite the dust. That was pure illusion. In reality, the same operational features can take up less layout space in O gauge hi-rail or tinplate because of the tighter turning radius of the track. To run most HO equipment, an 18-inch radius is required (creating a circle of track with a 36-inch diameter). O gauge tinplate track forms a 31-inch circle, and O-27 obviously has a 27-inch diameter. You figure it out. Although an HO layout in a given amount of space might have a more prototypical look, it could well be operationally inferior.

Ready-to-run equipment. This is a big advantage for people who are pressed for time or aren't particularly craft-oriented. Almost everything can be used as soon as it is taken out of the box. If you wish to modify it or add superdetails later, fine. That can be done at your leisure.

Reliability and durability: A few bumps and scrapes rarely bother the locomotives because they were designed for hard use in the hands of children. If you keep them lubricated, they keep on chugging. The positive coupling and uncoupling functions are reliable, and fewer derailments occur than with smaller trains.

Track cleaning and maintenance. Although periodic cleaning is recommended, toy trains are not as susceptible to problems caused by dirty track as their scale counterparts are. The expansion and contraction of the rails, due to seasonal variations in temperature and humidity, can raise havoc in smaller gauges. But O gauge is affected less because it is larger.

Simplified wiring. The electrical circuits are not as complicated with a three-rail track system.

Insulated track sections can be used to trigger accessories. Reverse loops require no special wiring or devices to maintain polarity. And insulated axles are not necessary, so locomotive and car wheels are less likely to come loose and cause trouble.

These are some of the advantages to the hi-rail route in model railroading. The others become evident as you go along. Having passed through a number of phases during my years in the hobby, I have become an ardent hi-rail advocate.

A PERSONAL MEMOIR

So many rites of passage await us on the road to maturity. When we reach a certain age, we are expected to put aside childish pursuits and pastimes and take up more adult ones. People of my generation who wanted to remain in the train hobby had to trade in their toys for scale models when they reached adolescence or risk ostracism. That was the norm of socially acceptable behavior. In my case, I literally swapped my prewar Lionel and American Flyer trains for jazz records. I was a "happening" kid. But the cylinder oil in my bloodstream didn't allow me to stay away from trains for too long.

Back then, HO was coming into vogue, so I was attracted to that scale. There was a ruggedly individualistic, pioneering spirit moving through the hobby at the time. Nothing was available ready to run. The kits on the market required a small machine shop and the patience of a saint to assemble. Almost every part had to be drilled, sawed, or filed to fit. Track was laid by hand. Much had to be improvised or built from scratch. The ability to tackle such formidable projects without giving up separated the men from the boys. Those of us who fancied ourselves men soon realized there was yet another division within that category: those who had only two thumbs and those who had more.

Everything was so labor-intensive that few of us were willing to admit that the results often did not measure up to our expectations. So we had to be creative in another way—we learned to rationalize away malfunctions. Why wouldn't the train work whenever anyone was watching? Why should it derail or uncouple every few feet, even on straight and level track? How could a fly speck on the rail stop the Broadway Limited? We spent much of our time dreaming up excuses for such aberrant phenomena.

Maintenance and repairs took up a large chunk of time, so there was little left for operation. That was probably just as well. For someone who grew up running his toy trains long and often, HO scale model railroading was a big disappointment. I yearned for my old trains, but they were gone. Oh well, I still had the jazz records.

The part of HO railroading that I enjoyed most was scratchbuilding cars. I guess that's because they were decorative and weren't expected to work. In all, I built more than a hundred of them. I suspected something was wrong when I found myself looking through my old Lionel catalogs for ideas on how to paint them.

My HO layout was never really finished. It wasn't long before it grew cobwebs and a layer of dust. Have you noticed how HO trains actually look more realistic when they get dusty? I had the most realistic trains in the state! Eventually, the benchwork succumbed to the crowbar, and I sold the trains. With the money, I bought some old Lionel pieces and started again. The cycle was complete.

The moral of the story: Don't waste 10 or 15 years of your life being frustrated, trying to prove that you have an adult hobby, before you experience the real fun of playing with trains. Go ahead. Do it now!

Toy trains aren't just for kids anymore.

EVERYTHING ELSE COLLECTORS AND OPERATORS NEED TO KNOW

I. BASIC TERMINOLOGY

Benchwork. The supporting structure upon which a model railroad is built.

Clockwork ("wind-up") locomotive. Any toy locomotive that uses a coil spring for power; usually hand-wound with a removable key. The energy created when the spring unwinds is transmitted to the locomotive wheels through a series of gears, similar to those found in spring-driven clocks.

Decal lettering. Logos or lettering printed on a thin transparent film that is transferred and pressed in place on the surface of a model.

Dry-transfer lettering. Commonly used in model restoration to simulate the rubber- or heat-stamped original. The lettering is applied by rubbing the back of its holding sheet, thereby transferring it to the surface of a model.

E-unit. The sequence-reverse mechanism found in Lionel locomotives.

Factory errors. Examples of the kind of mistakes that sometimes happen in any manufacturing operation and were not caught by quality control. Although some errors may involve a number of units, they are goofs, not variations.

Factory prototypes and/or samples. Preproduction models intended for use by executives and employees to help visualize new product designs or improvements in the line.

Gauge. The distance between the running rails of model train track. It is usually expressed in letters, such as G, O, HO, N, and Z, and is commonly confused with scale, which is sometimes entirely different. O gauge track, for example, has 1.25 inches between the running rails.

Heat-stamped lettering. Lettering applied with colored foil and a hot press. Because of the heat, this lettering is often slightly indented into the surface of the model.

Hi-railers. Modelers who operate stock tinplate trains in scale-like, highly detailed, and often fully scenicked settings.

Layout. A common term for a model railroad or operating train display.

Pike. A common term for a model railroad (also a fish found in northern Wisconsin).

Power pack. An electrical device that reduces 110-volt house current to lower voltages and converts them to DC (direct current) usable to power model trains. Power packs are more commonly used with scale model railroads.

Prototype. Term that usually refers to the full-sized trains after which the models are patterned.

Railfans. People who love trains of all kinds, whether they are looking at them, riding on them, or talking about them.

Representation. A model train that is painted and lettered to represent something that it was not originally. This is usually done by collectors who want to fill in a gap that should be occupied by a rare and/or unusual piece that might be difficult or impossible to find.

Reproduction. A model train patterned after an antique that is long out of production. A good reproduction should be faithful to the original in shape, color, and materials used.

Restoration. A model train that is returned to its original condition by carefully repairing and repainting it.

Roadbed. In prototype railroading this is usually gravel or crushed stone over which the tracks are laid. Roadbed can be modeled in a variety of ways, but it most often consists of some flat material that supports the track at an elevation slightly above the surrounding terrain.

Rolling stock. A term from real railroad equipment rosters. It covers both locomotives and cars.

Rubber-stamped lettering. Inked letters or numbers applied to models with a rubber stamp similar to those in many offices.

Scale. A proportion or comparative ratio of a model's measurements to the dimensions of the full-sized prototype train. For example, O scale is a 1:48 proportion, which means that 1 inch on the model's surface represents 48 inches on the prototype. This can also be expressed as ¼″ = 1′.

Scale model railroaders. People who build (or intend to build) highly detailed, exact scale miniaturizations of some portion of the real world, with railroading as the central focus. Many of these individuals are creative and industrious and have a great diversity of artistic and manual skills that they constantly apply. Others are content to manage things from their armchairs.

Swap meet. A gala periodic event, usually sponsored by a model train organization, patronized by hobbyists intent on buying and selling train-related items. In spite of the name, little "swapping" actually goes on.

TCA standards. A system of grading used trains, having several categories or ranges of condition. Helpful when buying or selling trains. These standards were devised and adopted by the Train Collectors Association.

Tinplate. A generic term commonly used to cover toy trains and related accessories of all kinds. It springs from the fact that the track upon which these trains run is made of tin-plated steel.

Train collectors. People infected with a highly contagious disease for which there is no known cure. Once stricken, their lives change completely.

Transformer. An electrical device that reduces 110-volt house current to lower AC voltages usable to power model trains.

Variations. Minor changes that were sometimes made in a particular piece or set over time. They often involve differences in color, lettering, or detailing that reflect changes in the manufacturing process over the years. The catalog number remains the same.

II. Toy and Model Train Associations

American Flyer Collectors Club
P. O. Box 13269
Pittsburgh, PA 15243

Ives Train Society
P. O. Box 32017
Richmond, VA 23226

K-Line Collectors Club
P. O. Box 2831
Chapel Hill, NC 27515

Lionel Collectors Club of America
P. O. Box 479
La Salle, IL 61301

Lionel Operating Train Society
P. O. Box 62240
Cincinnati, OH 45241

Lionel Railroader Club
P. O. Box 748
New Baltimore, MI 48047

Marx Train Collectors Club
P. O. Box 111
Bakerstown, PA 15007

MTH Railroaders Club
7020 Columbia Gateway Dr.
Columbia, MD 21046

National Association of S Gaugers
Mike Ferraro
280 Gordon Rd.
Matawan, NJ 07747

National Model Railroad Association
4121 Cromwell Rd.
Chattanooga, TN 37421

Toy Train Collectors Society
Louis A. Bohn
109 Howedale Dr.
Rochester, NY 14616

Toy Train Operating Society
25 W. Walnut St.
Suite 408
Pasadena, CA 91103

Train Collectors Association
P. O. Box 248
Strasburg, PA 17579

III. MANUFACTURERS OF TOY TRAINS AND RELATED PRODUCTS

American Models
10087 Colonial Industrial Dr.
South Lyon, MI 48178

Arttista Accessories
1616 S. Franklin St.
Philadelphia, PA 19148

Atlas O
603 Sweetland Ave.
Hillside, NJ 07205

Bachmann Industries Inc.
1400 E. Erie Ave.
Philadelphia, PA 19124

Bowser Manufacturing Co.
P. O. Box 322
Montoursville, PA 17754

Dallee Electronics Inc.
10 Witmer Rd.
Lancaster, PA 17602

Depotronics Inc.
P. O. Box 2093-B
Warrendale, PA 15086

GarGraves Trackage Corp.
P. O. Box 255-A
North Rose, NY 14516

Hartland Locomotive Works
P. O. Box 1743
LaPorte, IN 46350

Korber Models
2 Tidswell Ave.
Medford, NJ 08055

L&J Hobbies
8847 Portage Rd.
Portage, MI 49002

LGB of America
6444 Nancy Ridge Dr.
San Diego, CA 92121

Lionel LLC
50625 Richard W. Blvd.
Chesterfield, MI 48051

Märklin Inc.
P. O. Box 510559
New Berlin, WI 53151-0559

Marx Trains
209 E. Butterfield Rd., No. 228
Elmhurst, IL 60126

MDK Inc.
P. O. Box 2831
Chapel Hill, NC 27515

Miami Valley Products Co.
1723 Lockbourne Dr.
Cincinnati, OH 45240

Model Rectifier Corp.
P. O. Box 6312
Edison, NJ 08818

MTH Electric Trains
7020 Columbia Gateway Dr.
Columbia, MD 21046

QSIndustries
3800 S.W. Cedar Hills Blvd., No. 224
Beaverton, OR 97005

Ross Custom Switches
P. O. Box 110
North Stonington, CT 06359

S-Helper Service Inc.
2 Roberts Rd.
New Brunswick, NJ 08901-1621

Third Rail
Sunset Models Inc.
37 S. Fourth St.
Campbell, CA 95008

United Model Distributors
301 Holbrooke Dr.
Wheeling, IL 60090

USA Trains
P. O. Box 100
662 Cross St.
Malden, MA 02148

Weaver Quality Craft Models
P. O. Box 231
RR 1
Northumberland, PA 17857

Williams Electric Trains
8835-F Columbia 100 Pkwy.
Columbia, MD 21045

IV. SELECTED BOOKS ON TOY TRAINS

Unless noted, all books are published by Kalmbach Publishing Co. Check with your local hobby shop for availability. You can also order the Kalmbach titles by phoning 1-800-533-6644, or you can order them online at http://books.kalmbach.com

A. C. Gilbert's Heritage (Heimburger House Publishing Co.)

All Aboard! The Story of Joshua Lionel Cowen & His Lionel Toy Train Company (Workman Publishing)

Beginner's Guide to Repairing Lionel Trains

Easy Lionel Layouts You Can Build

Greenberg's Guide to American Flyer S Gauge, vol. 1

Greenberg's Guide to Lionel Trains 1901–1942, vols. 1–4

Greenberg's Guide to Lionel Trains 1945–1969, vols. 1, 3, 4, and 6

Greenberg's Repair and Operating Manual for Lionel Trains: 1945–1969

Greenberg's Wiring Your Lionel Layout, vols. 1–3

How to Build Your First Lionel Layout

Lionel: A Collector's Guide and History, vols. 1–6 (Chilton Book Co.)

Realistic Plastic Structures for Toy Trains

Realistic Railroading with Toy Trains

Realistic Scenery for Toy Train Layouts

Realistic Track Plans for O Gauge Trains

The World's Greatest Toy Train Maker: Insiders Remember Lionel

Tips and Tricks for Toy Train Operators

Track Plans for Toy Trains

INDEX